GIRL TALK

WORDS EVERY WORLD-CHANGING GIRL NEEDS TO HEAR

KATIE ZEPPIERI

Make Your Mark Enterprises Ltd.

GIRL TALK

Note from the author: Some names have been changed in this book to protect the privacy of the individuals involved.

First Edition

Edited by: Shawn Byron Beckett
Book Design by: Madison Hayhoe
Cover Photos by: Purple Canvas Photography

Font Illustration by: Lauren Thompson (Champagne & Limousines)

Written & compiled in Canada. Printed in the United States of America.

ISBN 978-1-329-36280-2

Published July 2015

Make Your Mark Enterprises Ltd.
910 Dundas St. W
P.O. #10012
Whitby, ON L1P 1P7

To every girl who has ever wanted to change the world,

this book is for you.

CONTENTS

FOREWORD

By Television Personality, Tanya Kim

I had the honour of hosting the 2015 GIRL TALK Empowerment Day in June and from the minute I walked onto that stage, I knew I was in for an unforgettable and incredible day. The positive energy from the 1400 girls in attendance was overwhelmingly palpable. It was exhilarating to witness so many young girls so excited to be part of a movement that inspires and motivates women of all different sizes, ages, and backgrounds.

Born one in a handful of Koreans and raised in a small town in Northern Ontario, Sault Ste. Marie to be exact, I experienced some challenging times. Being bullied was the most hurtful. As you can imagine, looking "different" wasn't exactly a quality that was embraced by everyone.

But I had dreams. Big ones. I always knew I wanted to work in the arts and entertainment world. On one hand, I wanted to follow in the footsteps of my brother Richard, who is an uber-talented dancer. Watching him work for his dream and achieve incredible success—he's worked with Michael Jackson, Gloria Estefan, Reba McEntire, just to name a few—I was especially inspired. But on the other hand, I was extremely fascinated by the media. When I was just a little kid, I used to watch magazine news shows like Primetime Live, 20/20 and Dateline with my mom. I also had an appreciation for reporters Barbara Walters and Oprah Winfrey. Their conversation-style resonated with me and that's how my love for "the conversation" began. But being the little girl who was made fun of for being different, it was a struggle at times to imagine my dreams becoming reality. On top of that, there was really nobody on television that I could relate to or that looked like me.

I took the challenge head on and I refused to let any little voice of doubt, insecurity or fear stop me from dreaming big and "going for it!" If you have a passion and a positive "can do" spirit, anything is possible.

I am blessed to be guided by a strong woman who always encourages me to do whatever it is I dream of doing. My mother is the woman in my life that reminds me to carve out my own path and keep going regardless of what obstacles I may face. She is my rock and biggest cheerleader (Love you, Mom!). This is the spirit of the GIRL TALK Empowerment movement, multiplied by a thousand. Founder Katie Zeppieri asked me to host the 2015 GIRL TALK Empowerment Day because she said I am an inspiration to many young girls out there and no doubt have some wisdom to offer. Funny thing is, I believe it was me who left that day feeling more inspired and empowered than ever.

It is invigorating and always refreshing to be in a room filled with so much support, love and positivity. My experience with being bullied as a young girl was difficult but it taught me to be more compassionate and to always choose kindness. As girls and women, let's look out for one another and be each other's biggest fans. I am grateful that I was able to experience this firsthand at the 2015 GIRL TALK Empowerment Day and I'm honoured to continue to be part of this movement. As Katie says, the world needs more "world-changers." I'm confident this book will inspire many of you to want to help make this planet of ours an even better place. "Keep It Shiny" friends, and remember, life is beautiful when we choose kindness!

INTRODUCTION

What Does it Mean to be a World-Changer?

There was a time when I used to think that I had to wait until I was a full-grown, successful adult before I could be a world-changer. I remember sitting in my room thinking about how great it would be when I had all the money in the world and a position of power. I'd think to myself: *Someday if I'm rich and powerful I'll donate to every single charity, adopt hundreds of animals and finally have my voice heard. Only then will I be able to truly make a difference.*

My opinion on what it means to change the world transformed when I witnessed an injustice in seventh grade. I was kicking around a soccer ball during recess when I noticed a group of my peers surrounding a girl from the special education class. At first glance, it was hard to tell exactly what was going on but as I moved closer I could see the look of distress on the girl's face. She had been known to struggle with anger and I would sometimes see her being counselled by teachers to help her deal with stress. But today she looked especially upset. She was pacing back and forth vigorously and waving her hands in the air. The small group of my classmates seemed to be enjoying the reaction they were getting from this girl and continued to mock her. They were calling her names, imitating her movements and laughing at all of her reactions. She was crying and yelling at the group to go away and leave her alone.

As I saw the look of complete despair cross the girl's face, I knew that I couldn't remain silent. My heart pounded hard in my chest as I took a deep breath and moved inside of the circle of kids. "Leave her alone!" I shouted, "Can't you see she's upset?" Everyone's eyes turned to me. My classmates weren't impressed with my interruption and started calling me a few names too. But I can't even remember what was said to me because my eyes met those of the poor girl I had just defended. It felt as though time stopped for a moment—it was a surreal experience where I saw her expression transform from hopelessness to hope. My stomach filled with butterflies and I could feel goosebumps all over. Slowly, the would-be bullies began backing away and finally, they were gone.

I'll never forget the way that girl looked at me on that fall afternoon. I knew that I wanted to fill my life with more of these feel-good moments where I had the courage to stand up against injustices and spread love and kindness. Suddenly changing the world didn't seem like such an unreachable goal. Sure, I might not be able to change everything about the world, but I certainly could change *my* world. I could choose to be a leader, to stand up for what is right and to seek to find a solution to every problem I encounter. And along the way, maybe, just maybe, my words and actions might be able to change someone else's world for the better.

This book is dedicated to every girl who has ever wanted to change the world. Being a world-changer is not without its challenges and sometimes the problems of the world can seem overwhelming. If you turn on any news station for a few minutes you will get a glimpse of the trials our world is facing: hunger, poverty, disease, war and environmental changes—just to name a few. Young people, both boys and girls, have the power to fix these problems in our world. But girls today face problems of their own. Our image-obsessed society tells girls that they can't change the world because they are not skinny, pretty, or talented enough. It's no wonder girls are struggling with their self-esteem and self-worth. It's time to make a shift.

The time has come for us to rally together and support one another. It's time for us to see our potential to make a difference in the world. It's time that we recognize that each of us can be a world-changer right where we are. As the saying goes, "To the world you might just be one person, but to one person you might just be the world."

CHAPTER 1

Who Am I to Make a Difference?

"I am only one, but I am one. I cannot do everything, but I can do something. And I will not let what I cannot do interfere with what I can do."
—Edward Everett Hale

I am not the best swimmer, especially in outdoor pools. It's not because I *can't* swim—I worked all the way up to the Level 12 badge, albeit with a nose plug—but because I am always distracted by insects drowning in the pool. Have you ever noticed the ants, flies, spiders and other many-legged critters that inevitably make their way into swimming pools? If you turn your back for even a minute, you'll find some new insect foolishly making its way into the water, not realizing that it is dancing on the edge of life and death. The little bug creeps slowly down the pool liner and then, at the first touch of water, is swept into the depths, never to reach dry land again. These poor insects swerve and struggle to try to find dry surfaces to grab onto but the majority of them never make it back to safety.

Call me crazy (trust me, many have), but I can't help but feel like I have some sort of moral duty to rescue these helpless creepy crawlers—even though I have a deathly fear of spiders! (More about fears later). I use leaves, branches and pool noodles to scoop up the insects and lift them to the pool deck. When I don't have any tools nearby I simply cup my hands and lift the insect up within a handful of water. I find great joy in seeing an insect find its way back onto its legs and continue scurrying along back to its ground-level life.

To a person watching me in the pool, what I am doing looks clearly ridiculous. I have been questioned and teased for insect-saving many times. "See how some of the insects go back down to the water even after you save them?" they say, "You can't possibly save all of them—what difference do you really think you're making?" To which I respond, as I cup my hands together and lift another ant out onto the pool deck, "I bet I made a difference to that one."

A common first thought that often goes through a young person's mind when they are told that they have the power to change the world is, "*Who am I to make a difference? I'm too young or unqualified to actually do anything world-changing.*" It's true that the phrase "Making a Difference" sounds a little too big to comprehend. We all have a classic idea of what being a world-changer really looks like. We picture people like prime ministers, world leaders and celebrities influencing and inspiring mass groups of people. We might also picture astronauts landing on the moon, athletes breaking world-records and scientists discovering cures for diseases. We picture the big stuff, the exciting stories. And while aspiring to achieve this level of greatness is something I want for all of us, I think it is also important to remember that we can be world-changers and difference-makers right where we are.

More than a Catchphrase

"You Can Make a Difference" has become a popular catchphrase used to encourage young people to see their full potential. Walk through almost any Canadian school or community centre and you will see inspirational messages reminding you to never give up and to chase your dreams. These messages are often embellished with epic pictures of people climbing mountains or sprinting towards a finish line. And while these posters are meant to be positive reinforcements, I believe that this large-scale imagery might appear intimidating to a young person just starting out on their journey. This intimidation is what can cause us to focus on the obstacles ahead of us and believe that we are too small to change the world.

Once doubt has entered the mind, the three main obstacles that stop people from reaching their goals begin to appear: **1) Excuses**, **2) Fears**, and **3) Roadblocks**. Excuses are the voices telling you that your goal is unreachable or that it is not even worth the effort. Fears are the worries of negative outcomes that creep into the forefront of our thinking. And finally, roadblocks are the external circumstances that happen to us on our way to reaching our goals. All of these obstacles provide their own unique set of challenges and are necessary to overcome on your path to making a difference and changing the world. As Michael Jordan once said, "Obstacles don't have to stop you. If you run into a wall, don't turn around and give up. Figure out how to climb it, go through it, or work around it."

Unfriend Excuses

Excuses are like lead weights that cling to your dreams and weigh them down, making them feel heavy and unlikely. They are the easiest substitute for hard work and arrive almost immediately after a new idea, goal or dream forms in our head. They are the "ifs," "ands" and "buts" we insert to give ourselves reasons not to do something.

Sometimes we befriend excuses because it feels comfortable to have a justification for why we cannot achieve our goal—even if that justification is untrue. The problem is that repeating our excuses to ourselves again and again clutter our mind with doubt and hold us back from reaching our true potential.

We need to take a stand and unfriend excuses so that they no longer have the power to control our thoughts. The best way to defeat excuses is to address each one as it enters your mind with a world-changer reality check, which will remind you of your own possibility and lift off those weights so you can soar.

EXCUSE	REALITY
"I'm too young."	Age is not a relevant factor when it comes to being a difference-maker. A five year-old that shares her lunch with a classmate who forgot their lunch makes a difference. A fifteen year-old who comes home early after school to babysit her sister makes a difference. No matter how young you may be, there is always something you can do to make the world a better place. Just take a look around you.
"I don't have enough experience."	Experience is gained daily by the actions we take. If you always say you can't try something new because you don't have any experience you never will try anything new and earn experience! You can't gain experience from the sidelines; you need to dive into the spotlight and learn as you go.

EXCUSE	REALITY
"I'm not good enough."	Everyone starts somewhere. Many world-changers once felt not good enough but chose to believe that they had the power to make a difference, and let their belief carry them towards their goals. By choosing to believe that you have the power to change the world around you, your perspective will shift to realize that you are placed right where you are because you have everything you need to make a difference.
"I don't have enough money."	Although having some money may be necessary to live in modern society, it is not necessary for making a difference in someone's life. Kindness doesn't cost a thing. We have an unlimited supply of kindness to offer those around us and we should choose to spread it like peanut butter. (Mmm...peanut butter).
"I don't have enough time."	You have just as many hours in a day as anybody else. World-changers prioritize their days to make time for the things that truly matter. If something is important to you, you will make time for it.

Flipping Fears

Fears are worries that linger in the back of our minds and cause us to question our abilities. Fears are brought to the forefront when we seek to try something new. These can range from skill-related fears such as a fear of public speaking, to goal-related fears such as a fear of not getting elected to student council.

One of the most common fears experienced by successful people is the fear of being accused of being a fake. This fear is better known as Imposter Syndrome—the feeling that you are a fraud and that someday you will be exposed as not being good enough. The incredible thing about Imposter Syndrome is that even the most high-achieving people can still feel this not-good-enough anxiety. Award-winning author, Maya Angelou, explained that even after achieving wide recognition, she still questioned herself: "I have written eleven books, but each time I think 'uh-oh, they're going to find [me] out now.'"

Being afraid to try something new is a natural part of the process of taking risks. We need to remind ourselves that everybody experiences fears. What sets leaders and world-changers apart is the ability to feel the fear and accomplish their goal anyway. It's important to address self-defeating attitudes as soon as they enter your mind. Instead of saying things like, "Anyone could have done this," say, "I worked hard for this."

FEARS	REASSURANCE
What if I fail?	You'll be one step closer to succeeding. As the great inventor, Thomas Edison said: "I have not failed. I've just found 10,000 ways that won't work."
What if people don't like me?	Not everyone is going to love you or support you in your journey. What matters most is that you love yourself and surround yourself with people who believe in your dreams.
What if I don't live up to expectations?	Your biggest expectation should be to always try your best. It's not the outcome that matters most—it's what you gained from the experience.

FEARS	REASSURANCE
What if someone else does it better?	The only person you should try to be better than is the person you were yesterday. Comparing yourself to others is a negative habit that will leave you feeling inadequate. Everyone has a unique set of talents and skills. Just because someone else is successful in one area does not mean your own personal success is diminished.
What happens after I succeed?	Reaching one goal is just the beginning of a new goal. One of the great joys of life is knowing that there is always something more to work towards and achieve.

New York Times best-selling author, Marianne Williamson, believes that what people truly fear more than anything else is, surprisingly, not doing poorly but doing too well. It is possible, she writes, for us to feel afraid of what will happen if we shine too bright. Below is an excerpt from one of her most famous books, *A Return to Love*:

> *Our deepest fear is not that we are inadequate. Our deepest fear is that we are powerful beyond measure. It is our light, not our darkness that most frightens us. We ask ourselves, Who am I to be brilliant, gorgeous, talented, fabulous? Actually, who are you not to be? You are a child of God. Your playing small does not serve the world. There is nothing enlightened about shrinking so that other people won't feel insecure around you. We are all meant to shine, as children do. We were born to make manifest the glory of God that is within us. It's not just in some of us; it's in everyone. And as we let our own light shine, we unconsciously give other people permission to do the same. As we are liberated from our own fear, our presence automatically liberates others.*

Ultimately, we have the power to face our fears and find the courage to pursue our dreams beyond the resistance. At the end of the day, **FEAR** can have two different meanings: 1) **F**orget **E**verything **A**nd **R**un; or, 2) **F**ace **E**verything **A**nd **R**ise. The choice is up to us.

Swerve Around Roadblocks

Even when you have unfriended excuses and decided to face your fears, there are still obstacles that may arise on your journey to become a world-changer. Whereas excuses and fears exist within our minds, roadblocks are the external forces that pose a challenge to us achieving our goals.

Roadblocks are unique challenges because we cannot control when and where they might happen to us. One day you could be on-track to achieving a goal and the next day you could have a major setback appear that forces you to change your original plan.

EXAMPLES OF ROADBLOCKS

- A person who was a vital part of a project you were leading drops out at the last minute.
- $ Your parent loses their job so now you have to drop out of an expensive extracurricular activity.
- + You've been training hard for an athletic competition and two weeks before the event you sprain your ankle.
- Someone you care about disapproves of your goal or dream.

All of these examples showcase scenarios where an unexpected turn of events could challenge a person's plan and force them to question whether or not their dream is still worth pursuing. These are the tests that challenge us to dig deeper and push harder. Roadblocks are difficult for even the most seasoned leader. There is nothing easy about having to re-direct a path so that it goes in a different direction yet still meets the same goal. Although we cannot choose what happens to us, we *can* choose how we respond to the roadblocks that come our way.

Roadblocks are one of the greatest tests any world-changer will ever face. These unforeseen challenges can sweep you off your feet when you least expect it and may cause you to go through a period of doubt. To be a leader is to recognize that roadblocks are bound to come your way at some point along your journey. Roadblocks can serve as springboards that propel you down a new path that might not have been in your original plan, but often lead to better outcomes than you could have imagined. As author Zig Ziglar once said, "When obstacles arise, you change your direction to your goal; you do not change your decision to get there."

NAVIGATING ROADBLOCKS

1	Take a deep breath and choose to respond in a calm manner. You will be able to think more clearly if you try to relax instead of getting upset.
2	Consider possible solutions for how to work around the challenge presented. Perhaps you will be able to still stay with the original timeline for your goal or maybe you will have to consider postponing to a later time.
3	Make a list of what resources you might need to achieve your goal.
4	Ask the people you trust for help and share with them what resources you are going to need to overcome the roadblock. They may just provide a boost of insight or inspiration that will make you see the situation differently.
5	Keep your eyes focused on your goal and remind yourself that things will happen when they are meant to happen.

That Little Extra

One of my all-time favourite quotes is by Jimmy Johnson, who said, "The difference between ordinary and extraordinary is that little 'extra.'" I love this quote because it reminds me that to be a world-changer and difference-maker doesn't mean that I have to do large-scale things; it just means that I need to put a little extra effort, kindness, love and determination into everything that I do. Whether it's holding open a door for someone, offering to carry groceries for a senior citizen or even saving ants from my family's swimming pool, I can make a difference, and so can you. After unfriending excuses, flipping fears and swerving roadblocks we need to choose to find our courage to break free from the status quo—the ordinary—and choose to live a life of EXTRAordinary leadership. It's the little extras that make all the difference.

DISCUSSION QUESTIONS

Chapter One: Who Am I to Make a Difference?

1) Have you ever worried that you were too young or unqualified to change the world? How did you overcome this worry?

2) What does "Make a Difference" mean to you?

3) List some more examples of Excuses people use for why they can't make a difference, then give each Excuse a world-changer Reality Check for why they can make a difference.

4) Have you ever experienced the feeling of Imposter Syndrome? Describe the experience.

5) What do you think is the biggest challenge young people face when they are working towards accomplishing a goal?

6) Take a look at the Fears & Reassurance chart. Can you relate to any of the Fears listed? How does reading the Reassurance make you feel?

7) Name a time where you experienced a Roadblock. How did you manage to overcome it?

8) How can you add a little "extra" into your life to make it EXTRAordinary? Name one thing each that you can do at school, home, and in your local community to make a positive difference.

Challenge for the Week

Make a list of any Excuses, Fears or Roadblocks that you face this week and then beside each item write a note of inspiration to yourself for how you can overcome the obstacle.

CHAPTER 2

The Problem with #FirstWorldProblems

"We can't solve problems by using the same kind of thinking we used when we created them."
—Albert Einstein

"I'VE GOT 99 PROBLEMS...
THAT AREN'T ACTUALLY SERIOUS PROBLEMS."

"I don't have enough dip for my chips. But if I open another container I won't have enough chips for my dip."

"My phone battery is dying but my charger is all the way upstairs."

"I should probably go exercise but my hair looks really good today and I don't want to ruin it."

"There isn't any food; there are just ingredients to make food."

"When your nail polish clashes with your lip colour."

What is a #FirstWorldProblem?

The Oxford English Dictionary defines a "First World Problem" as a "relatively trivial or minor problem or frustration, implying a contrast with a serious problem such as those that may be experienced in the developing world." This slang term became a popular Internet meme beginning in 2005 on social media sites and soon became a common hashtag on Instagram, Twitter and other social networks. At the time of this publishing the #FirstWorldProblems hashtag has been used over 992,000 times on Instagram and thousands more times on Twitter.

What's the Problem?

Admittedly, I don't believe that too many people actually consider chip/dip ratios or clashing colours to be genuine problems. #FirstWorldProblems are not so much problems as they are complaints about minor inconveniences. It suggests that the world is divided into two categories: the privileged, in wealthy countries; and the less privileged, in developing countries. Using this hashtag draws a thick line of separation between privileged and non-privileged communities, ironically drawing attention to the mild annoyances of life in the developed world.

So what's the problem with #FirstWorldProblems? I believe there are two main problems: 1) It celebrates laziness; and 2) It promotes entitlement. Does having the colour of your nail polish clash with the colour of your lipstick really pose a major obstacle to your ability to make the world better today? Probably not, and by taking the time to complain about it, not only are you wasting your time, but the time of those who read about it. In the time we spend complaining about how far away our phone charger is from our current location, we could've already gotten the charger and begun doing more productive things with our time.

Problem One: Celebrating Laziness

In the past two hundred years or so, industrialized Western society has developed at a rapid pace. Agriculture, healthcare, communications and housing are just a few of the many industries that have dramatically evolved to make living standards much higher for the average twenty-first century North American citizen than for her ancestors.

Many of our great, great, great, great, great, great grandparents had to work hard to secure even the basic necessities for living. For instance, many had to operate their own farms so that they could harvest food for their family to eat, and the teenagers living at home would have more than likely been a part of this process. Chores like feeding chickens, milking cows and picking vegetables from the garden would have all been routine parts of meal preparation. Putting food on the table was a daily struggle.

Today, for the middle class, food is everywhere. Fast food restaurants are on most major intersections, pre-made meals have become commonplace and we can have almost any fruit or vegetable we like, even when it is out of season. Just a few decades ago, getting food to eat would have required hours of preparation—today, for those of us in Canada and the developed world, it can take as little as two minutes (depending on how far you live from Tim Horton's or McDonald's!).

Surely, all of this extra time that modern living affords us could be used to improve our lives and the lives of those around us. But instead, we spend our time staring at screens and airing our complaints about minor inconveniences. Complaining makes us passive, and passivity prevents us from being world-changers. Changing the world involves taking action. Action requires us to break free of celebrating laziness and move from being problem-focused critics to solution-focused leaders.

Problem Two: Promoting Entitlement

Another problem with #FirstWorldProblems is that it promotes entitlement. Who ever said that we were owed the conveniences that we take for granted? The world doesn't owe us anything; we already have all of the necessary resources for survival. As human beings, it's *our* responsibility to ensure that people living in every corner of the globe have access to basic necessities to live and are treated with dignity and respect. This is a responsibility that I do not take lightly, and neither should you.

If we're too busy complaining about how difficult miniscule tasks are, how are we ever going to rise to the occasion to contribute something meaningful to the world? Instead of complaining that our iPhone is not the newest model anymore, we should be thankful that we even have cell phones in the first place. In Canada, over 80% of people own a mobile phone, most of which are Internet-enabled smartphones. Compare that to Cuba, arguably one of Canada's favourite tourist destinations, where only about 18% people have a cell phone, and practically no one has an Internet data plan.

When we complain about #FirstWorldProblems, we assume that our modern, industrialized country owes us a certain standard of luxury and comfort. Former United States President John F. Kennedy refuted that idea in his iconic 1961 speech: "Ask not what your country can do for you, ask what you can do for your country." I would like to extend this idea even further, by encouraging you to ask what you can do for the *world*.

Make the Switch from Problems to Solutions

If we're not helping to make it right then we need to stop complaining about it being wrong. I think it's important to remember that no matter where we are in our life journey there is always someone worse-off than we are, dealing with problems of larger magnitudes. The time has come to abandon the trend to talk about problems that don't matter and instead focus on creating solutions for the problems that do matter.

In 2014, our GIRL TALK Empowerment Team began launching inspiring media with the hashtag #FirstWorldSolutions, with the goal of getting young people to be part of the solution to some of the world's problems. This fresh take on a popular meme has made its appearance at our GIRL TALK Empowerment Days, on school speaking tours and even in a Toronto-based march against human-trafficking. The goal? Encourage young people to make the switch from identifying small problems to finding big solutions.

A problem is a problem that will always be a problem unless we do something to change it. #FirstWorldProblems give far too much attention and time to minor inconveniences, instead of talking about things that truly matter. Time is too precious a thing for world-changers to waste. We've got lots of work to do to make the world a better place for everyone to live and there's no time like the present to begin making changes. World-changers are people who solve problems without wasting time complaining about them.

DISCUSSION QUESTIONS

Chapter Two: The Problem with #FirstWorldProblems

1) Have you ever posted a #FirstWorldProblem on social media? What was it?

2) Why do you think the #FirstWorldProblems hashtag is so popular?

3) The author describes her experience of growing up as a young girl and noticing that her appearance seemed to become more important to the people around her as she got older. Did you experience a similar shift in others' perception of you? How did you cope with this?

4) Do you think our society "celebrates laziness"? Why or why not?

5) How can we show more appreciation for what we have?

6) What are some ways you can switch your mindset from focusing on problems to focusing on solutions?

Challenge for the Week

Post an inspiring way that we can make the world a better place and use the hashtag #FirstWorldSolutions.

CHAPTER 3

The Real Meaning of Beauty

"Beauty begins the moment you decide to be yourself."
—Coco Chanel

What would you say if I told you the most beautiful thing about you has absolutely nothing to do with how you look and everything to do with who you are? You might say something like, "Yeah right. I've never seen inner beauty celebrated on a magazine cover," and you'd have a point.

Growing up as a female in North America is like growing up looking in a defective mirror that highlights your flaws. Billboards, music videos, television shows, magazines and the World Wide Web fill our lives with repeated images of gorgeously captured girls and women. Girls in media are eye-candy and sex symbols who woo men with their feminine charms. From their flowing locks of hair to their full bust, small waist and long, tanned legs, we have a pretty clear idea of what it means to be beautiful—or at least we think we do.

The word "beauty" actually has a long history dating back to the fourteenth century, stemming from the Anglo-French word *beute*, meaning "goodness" or "courtesy." Goodness? Yes, the word beauty began as a synonym for goodness! This is how I like to see the word beauty being interpreted. When I say someone is beautiful, I'm choosing that word over "pretty," "hot," or any other physical descriptor, because beautiful to me is an inside-out term that encompasses the whole person—not only their physical features.

The truth of the matter is that our appearance is ever changing. We look differently when we're twelve, when we're eighteen, and when we're fifty. Everybody is born looking unique: from our skin colour to our eye shape to the curves of our cheekbones. For the most part, how we look is completely out of our control. Sure, we can load on makeup, dye our hair or even get surgical procedures done, but we still do not have full control over our appearance. The one thing that no human being can change is the fact that we age from year-to-year and decade-to-decade. No matter how much money we spend on the fanciest moisturizers or the most exotic facials, the inevitable will eventually happen: we will grow old. Does this mean that elderly people are not beautiful? Some superficial definitions of beauty say that this is so, but not our world-changing definition of beauty. To us, beauty is about so much more than what meets the eye.

World-changers look for beauty beyond skin deep. We believe that personal beauty should be about more than how you look. We cannot control the appearance we were born with but we can control the kind of human being we are. Choosing love over hate, courage over fear and kindness over jealousy is beautiful. Being a leader who stands up for the rights of others is beautiful. Working every day to make your dream come true is beautiful. And the most beautiful part of this definition of beauty? It's something we *all* can achieve.

The Pressure to Be Perfect

I was blessed to grow up in a loving family who nurtured and protected me from a young age. My parents were there to hear my every dream and always believed in me no matter what crazy idea I presented to them—and trust me, some were pretty crazy. This foundation of love gave me the confidence to believe that I really could achieve everything I hoped for. My parents told me that I was beautiful often and for a long time I believed them. And then Grade Seven came along.

When I hit the age of twelve, something strange began to happen. My breasts started to grow, my hips began to widen and within a year, I got my period. More than that, I suddenly became aware of the fact that my body was a point of interest to boys. Guys in my class would start to refer to girls' bodies as "sexy," some boys in the class would ask me what kind of underwear I was wearing, and online on MSN Messenger (the Snapchat of my day) boys would ask what my bra size was.

In addition to pressure from my peers, the media I watched also had a powerful effect on me. I would come home after school most days and turn on MuchMusic to see the top music videos of the week. These music videos would be filled with barely clothed girls and the camera shots would focus in on their lips, breasts and bums, leaving little to the imagination. I always wondered why I would feel down after watching these music videos, not realizing that the images being shown to me were seriously challenging my self-esteem.

The comparison game quickly began. I started to look at other girls and judge myself based on how they looked. Her boobs are so big, why don't mine look like that? That model makes those jeans look amazing, why don't jeans look good on me? She only weighs one hundred pounds, why am I so heavy? These comparisons hovered in my mind and affected the way that I looked at myself. Suddenly I saw myself as not good enough and unworthy of popularity. Although my parents continued to tell me I was beautiful it was much harder to believe. Many of my peers didn't think I was beautiful, and everywhere I looked I saw images of girls whom I believed to be more beautiful than me.

This pressure to be perfect is something that nearly all girls experience as they transition into womanhood. I realize that I am one of the girls on the privileged side of the spectrum. There are, sadly, many girls who are never told that they are beautiful and who feel that their dreams are discouraged. For these girls, the struggle to handle the pressure to be perfect is even harder. My hope is that by sharing some of my insecurities and experiences with you, I can encourage you to embrace what makes you unique and invite you to choose to love who you are—inside and out.

The Extent to Which Looks Matter

Unfortunately, I would be lying to you if I simply told you that looks don't matter. Human beings are visual animals, and use the appearance of other people to gain information about them. Imagine showing up to a job interview with messy hair or to a driving test wearing a bikini—I'm pretty sure those situations wouldn't turnout too well! We may not all have supermodel good looks, but making ourselves well-groomed and presentable goes a long way towards forming good first impressions. In short, I won't say that looks don't matter at all—they do. But they're not the most important things about us. Not by a long shot.

Girls face many challenges as they enter puberty. Suddenly, the world that we knew as a young girl drastically changes. Being a nice girl and a good student no longer seems to matter as much as looking pretty. It's right around the age of twelve that many of us start to feel curious about trying on makeup and dressing differently (hello bras!). We also begin to sense that being attractive is no longer just about our face, but also our bodies. This is the age where girls often start tweezing their eyebrows and shaving their legs in an effort to look more attractive.

As a half-Italian girl I can unapologetically say that I was born with a healthy serving of hair—which is celebrated on my head but is vilified on my body. It was jarring when my peers made me feel like the body hair with which I was born, suddenly needed to be removed. I actually cried the first time my mom shaved my legs in Grade Six because I felt like I was losing a piece of myself—which I guess I technically was. And then in Grade Eight I went to have my first professional makeup application at a salon, to practise for my graduation. The woman doing my makeup at the time felt compelled to tell me that I should consider getting my eyebrows "done" and that she'd be happy to wax them for me. *Um, thanks.*

From then on, I began getting my eyebrows waxed, and boy, did I go through some interesting stages! First, there was the *I'm-surprised-by-everything-all-the-time* brow stage, which was followed by the *I'm-always-really-angry* brow stage. The estheticians would wax and tweeze the heck out of my eyebrows until they were just thin, rounded lines that looked like the McDonald's arches. They told me how wonderful I looked with my eyebrows so thin. "All cleaned up now!" they'd say, but the truth was that this new look didn't feel like me or even really look like me. It took me a few years to realize that I actually preferred my eyebrows closer to their natural state—full and thick—with minimal shaping. And guess what everybody? Big eyebrows are IN! Look who's hip and happening now! (Hehe).

Yes, growing up in a world where everyone wants you to change the way that you look is tough. Sadly, there isn't one magical answer to address the many questions and challenges that us girls face as we enter our teen years. All I can say is that you need to do what feels right to you—period. Sure, the world might tell you to shave until you look like a naked mole rat and pile on mascara until your eyelashes touch your forehead, but if that doesn't feel right to you, or goes against your beliefs, then don't do it. This stage of life is all about choices and you have the right to choose what makes you feel beautiful. If you want to wear makeup, then wear makeup. If you don't want to wear makeup, then don't wear makeup. If you want to shave, then shave. If you don't want to shave, then don't shave. Whatever you choose for yourself, make sure that you choose for the right reasons and not because it lives up to someone's expectations of you.

At the end of the day, your looks are far from being the most important thing about you. I can spend all of my precious time straightening my hair, waxing my legs and putting on lipstick, but all it will do is alter my appearance. As fabulous as my straight hair, smooth legs and pink lips might be, they aren't going to do anything to change the world. We as world-changers need to be less concerned with the superficial, surface stuff (how we look), and more concerned about the difference we are making in the world (what we do). I love an Instagram post I saw the other week that said, "Mother Teresa didn't go around worrying about thigh gaps; she had stuff to do." Similarly, we all have a unique calling and purpose in this world, far beyond looking pretty, and we might just miss it if we don't pull ourselves away from the mirror and out into the world awaiting us.

More than Meets the Eye

One of the largest self-esteem challenges I have struggled with was coming to terms with my eye disorder. I was born with Duane syndrome, also called Duane retraction syndrome, a rare eye muscle disorder that causes abnormal eye movements. In 90% of Duane syndrome cases, the patient has no previous family history of Duane syndrome. I believe that I belong to the other 10%, as it was likely, though undiagnosed, that my dad's father had Duane syndrome as well. People born with Duane syndrome often have difficulty rotating one or both eyes outward or inward. Duane syndrome more commonly affects girls than boys, and in 80% of cases affects only one eye, usually the left eye, which is the case for me.

My Duane syndrome prohibits my left eye from moving towards my left ear, meaning that I am unable to keep my face forward and move both eyes to the left. If someone were to hold a pen and ask me to follow it with my eyes I'd be able to follow it up, down, and to the right but not fully to the left. When keeping my face forward but trying to move my eyes out to the left side, only my right eye moves and this makes me look cross-eyed. My Duane syndrome doesn't really have a major effect on my day-to-day activities, but it can cause some minor discomfort. When my eyes look crossed I can feel a deep strain in my left eye and it causes me to see double. If I hold a strained eye position for too long it gives me a headache and makes me feel dizzy. In order to look to the left, I'd have to fully turn my head, which releases pressure from my left eye.

My embarrassment about my Duane syndrome began the day friends and peers started asking what was wrong with my eye. As a particularly expressive and animated child I found it hard to hide my eye disorder. I remember the shame I would feel when someone pointed it out—especially in front of a group of people. In those moments when someone drew attention to my eye disorder I felt ugly. I had dreams of one day appearing on camera and speaking in front of large groups of people, but wondered how I was going to do all of these things if I had moments where I looked cross-eyed. Who would ever want to watch someone on television who made cross-eyed expressions like me?

My shame grew as I got older and entered high school. Questions about my eye were a regular occurrence and I could always feel myself getting defensive anytime someone asked why I looked cross-eyed. But these questions weren't nearly as confidence-crushing as the mockery of my disorder. In one instance, I remember sitting in my geography class in Grade Nine working on an assignment when one of the girls sitting in front of me called over to the girl sitting to my left and then made a cross-eyed face. They both looked at each other, then me, and laughed. Were they making fun of me? It seemed too obvious to be coincidental. These were girls that used to be my friends in elementary school and the teasing felt even more hurtful coming from them.

Another public confrontation about my Duane syndrome happened in Grade Eleven. I was walking up the stairs between periods three and four when I passed a friend-of-a-friend, an attractive boy a grade lower than me. We made eye contact and I felt a bit of a strain in my eye muscles and knew my Duane syndrome had shown itself. I hoped he didn't notice. "Are you cross-eyed?" he asked loudly. My heart sank. Is he actually going to make a scene? I kept walking. "Hey everybody, it's Katie the cross-eyed freak," he declared loudly, "There she goes!" I could hear my parents' voices in my head telling me to stand up for myself, but I just couldn't. I didn't know what to say.

Many nights, I came home crying when people pointed out my Duane syndrome. I found it hard to believe that my peers couldn't see just how much their words and actions hurt me. Over time, people drawing attention to my Duane syndrome became a trigger to pent-up emotions that I was repressing. I think all of us have a trigger word or action that really hurts us on a deeper level. It's the one flaw or criticism that lingers in our hearts long after the teasing has stopped. A trigger word can hit you at even the highest time in your life and it will still bring you right back to the little girl who came home crying after school. People can tell me my hair looks bad or that my nose is big or any other negative criticism, but it will never hit me quite as hard as when someone draws attention to the fact that I look cross-eyed from time to time.

Flipping Your "Flaws" for Good

I'd like to be able to tell you that I am now perfectly unhurt when someone makes a cross-eyed face or asks me about my eye, but that would not be the truth. I still find myself getting a bit sensitive when people ask me if I have a lazy eye. I often focus on keeping my head facing forwards whenever I am walking past someone in a hallway, as I know that if I try to make eye contact when they are in close proximity I will be looking at them cross-eyed. I worry that my look-straight-ahead behaviour makes me seem rude or snobbish, and I sometimes feel that my greetings can look inauthentic if I am caught off-guard and have to look to the left quickly. This is part of the scar tissue that I carry with me from the years of teasing and humiliation. Some people call the things that make us different flaws, abnormalities or even defects. And for a long time I saw these as a bad thing—something I needed to hide. It was only when

I chose to embrace my imperfections that I truly fell in love with myself and my life.

The biggest lesson I've learned from my journey with Duane syndrome is that the best form of acceptance comes when we have the courage to reveal who we truly are. For many years I felt like I needed to hide my Duane syndrome from the world as if it was some sort of unspeakable secret. Hiding my eye disorder was one of the worst choices I could have made for my self-esteem. By choosing to hide an important piece of me it stifled my development and became a self-imposed scar. Looking back, I realize that many of my peers might not have considered that I actually had a diagnosable eye disorder. And I'm quite sure that many of the people who asked me about my eye had good intentions. If I could go back, I think I would have been more assertive and unafraid to tell my friends that I had Duane syndrome. This might not have stopped the bullying, but it would have likely given me the confidence to stand up for myself. To a certain extent I think that I allowed myself to be victimized when I was bullied. I thought my Duane syndrome was ugly so when others made fun of my eyes it just reconfirmed what I already believed about myself. The moment I decided to see my eye disorder as a beautiful part of me was the moment I released the power I had given to the bullies and put the power of my self-worth back in my own hands.

I followed this same journey of acceptance with a scar on the left side of my back. When I was a baby, I had ureteral implant surgery—a fancy name for a surgery that reconnects your ureter (the tube that runs from your kidney to your bladder). Normally, the ureter works in such a way that urine is allowed to enter the bladder but not allowed to go back up to the kidney. When the ureter enters the bladder abnormally, urine flows back toward the kidney causing reflux—which can create serious health problems. Luckily, the doctors caught this problem early so that I could have the surgery and live a healthy life. I was, however, left with a four-inch scar on my back, just below the waist. I also have an even larger frontal scar on my lower abdomen from a vesicostomy (a surgery that creates an opening for urine to drain) because I wasn't able to empty my bladder when I was born. Once again I found myself viewing my scars as physical flaws that needed to be hidden. For many years I changed in closed-door bathrooms during gym class so that people wouldn't see my scars. I also remember consciously trying to pick bathing suits that would cover my back scar as I thought people would think my scar was unattractive. I freed myself from the chains of trying to hide pieces of me when I decided to celebrate my scars—which, need I mention, were after-effects of life-saving surgeries. Definitely something to celebrate!

I knew that I had made a drastic change in my self-acceptance when it came time for me to walk on-stage in a bathing suit at the 2013 Miss World Canada pageant. There have always been debates about whether or not it's oppressive for girls to wear bikinis on-stage as part of a pageant and I can see that argument, but for me it was truly liberating. Walking in my turquoise bathing suit on the Miss World Canada stage was a moment where I proved to myself that I had grown to love my body—every single part of it. I was a girl who always wore shorts at the beach because I thought my thighs were too big and who hid in bathroom changerooms to hide my scars. And there I was, walking in front of an audience to tell myself and the world that I was confident in who I was. The judges and the competition just seemed to fade into the background. I didn't care what other people thought about my body—I believed that I had every right to be on that stage just like all of the other girls—and that confidence made me feel beautiful.

Of course, walking on a stage in a bathing suit isn't the only way to feel beautiful. When we rise above our insecurities, and choose to love all of our quirks and imperfections, it's a beautiful feeling. I believe that we are given certain challenges in life so that we can grow into the person we are meant to be by overcoming them. My Duane syndrome has been an obstacle in self-acceptance for me over the years but I also believe it has been one of my greatest building blocks. I learned what it means to feel vulnerable and understood at a young age just how powerful hateful words could be. I believe that this understanding is what motivated me to be a champion for the underdogs of the world—the people who were overlooked or made to feel less than human because of their personality or appearance. My Duane syndrome and scars helped me feel compassion and empathy at a young age, which inspired me to stand up for others who were singled out as "different." If a surgery became available tomorrow that would take away my Duane syndrome, I wouldn't sign up for it. My eye disorder is part of what makes me, well, me. I wouldn't be the person I am today if I didn't have the experience of growing up with Duane syndrome and that experience has changed my life for the better.

Flowers in a Beautiful Garden

A flower doesn't think of competing with the flower next to it; it just blooms. We girls are all just flowers in a beautiful garden. Too often we see girls and women hating and becoming jealous of each other because of their own insecurities. We need to remember that just because someone else is pretty doesn't mean that we aren't pretty, and just because someone else is successful doesn't mean that we are unsuccessful. A sunflower is just as lovely as a rose and a daisy is just as lovely as a tulip. All of these flowers are different and beautiful in their own right.

Like flowers, someone else's beauty does not detract from our own beauty. Instead of seeing positive traits of others as negatives for ourselves, we need to celebrate and encourage one another. I like to look to inspiring females, who live confidently and compassionately, for inspiration. I seek out role models who I can relate to and admire the celebrities who use their status to do good works. When we see qualities in other girls whom we admire, we can choose to block out any feelings of jealousy and instead choose to empower them with our words and actions. Being a girl is tough sometimes and it sure would make life a lot easier if we all had each other's backs and encouraged one another to blossom into the beautiful individuals we are meant to be. After all, world-changers realize that they are the most beautiful when they are lifting up others, chasing their dreams and making a difference in the world.

DISCUSSION QUESTIONS

Chapter Three: The Real Meaning of Beauty

1) The word "beauty" originally stemmed from an Anglo-French word meaning "goodness." How do you think our society defines the meaning of beauty today?

2) Have you ever felt pressure to be perfect? Where did this pressure come from?

3) How do you feel when you look in the mirror? What are the positive things that you see?

4) The author describes the experience of growing up as a young girl and noticing that others thought of her appearance as being more important as she got older. Did you experience a similar shift in others' perception of you? How did you cope with this?

5) Do you believe that looks matter at all? To what extent?

6) In this chapter the author shares her experience of coming to terms with Duane syndrome, one of her most difficult self-esteem challenges. What has been the biggest self-esteem challenge you have faced?

7) Why do you think girls are quick to compare themselves to other girls?

8) After reading this chapter, has your definition of beauty changed? How so?

Challenge for the Week

Go out of your way to compliment other girls and women this week. Compliment them on their appearance, their personality, their style or any other positive trait that you like. Spread the love and watch how beautiful it will make you feel; you'll be glowing from the inside-out!

CHAPTER 4

Finding Your Passions

"Say yes and you'll figure it out afterwards."
—Tina Fey

I always knew that I wanted to live a full life. When I pictured myself in the future I imagined a happy, fulfilled and successful Katie. Images of me in a business suit, complete with fabulous heels (obviously), and working in an office are what came to mind. I also imagined leading meetings, speaking in front of crowds of people and running the show.

But wait a minute. I've got the outfit, I've got the setting…what show am I running exactly? What was missing from my vision was my passion—and this is the part that took many years to develop.

A passion is something that gets you ridiculously excited and motivated. I like to think of a passion as an interest so strong that it compels you to action. It's not enough just to like doing something. I like playing Mario Kart but that's probably not something I'd consider to be a lifelong passion (although it is a sweet Friday night pastime!).

The million-dollar question is: How exactly does a person find their passion? Like most million-dollar questions, there is not a one-size-fits-all answer. From my own experience, I have seen that following your curiosity is a great way to open yourself up to new opportunities. It is in the middle of opportunity that passions often spark. In this chapter I will share some of the experiences that helped me find my passions. I encourage you to say "yes" to taking risks, trying new things and staying committed to your goals.

Where the Magic Happens

I often refer to my dog, Max, when I think about the power of taking risks. Max is a ten year-old Shih Tzu who is extremely moody and prone to routine. A typical day in the life of Max involves waking up early to go outside, having a snack, and sleeping until the family returns home at the end of the day. Then he goes back outside and eats more snacks. This routine is within Max's comfort zone. If you try to pick him up during the middle of one of his cozy naps, he will usually growl to let you know that his slumber is not to be interrupted.

Generally speaking, Max likes his comfort zone. It's his daily routine and a safe schedule that guarantees him a degree of quiet contentment each day. There are two phrases, however, that send Max into fits of high-energy excitement. The first phrase that excites him is, "Time for a walk, Max!" At the mention of the word "walk," his eyes bulge open, his tail begins wagging and he immediately runs over to me and starts pawing at my legs, waiting for me to put on his leash.

The second phrase that excites my little pooch is, "Max! Car ride!" The idea of riding in a car sends Max into a state of simultaneous joy and terror. His eyes bulge open, his tail begins wagging and he immediately runs over to me, but then he stops in his tracks. Fear beings to creep into his little doggie brain, and he's not so sure he should be excited about a car ride.

You see, the magical car ride has two possible destinations: 1) The Lake, which in Max's eyes is pure pee-on-every-tree paradise; or 2) The Vet, also known as doggie prison. Each time I ask Max if he wants to go for a car ride (or as my family says, "car-car ride") both possible destinations circle in his mind and send him running towards me one moment and hurtling away from me the next. His contrasting emotions usually send him into a state of shakes where he stops running and jitters come over his body. Nine times out of ten when we say "car-car ride" we are taking Max for a walk by the lake. But it's that one out of ten chance of a trip to the vet that sends Max into a shaky state of paralysis.

The reality of the situation is that Max will never know if he is going to the lake or to the vet until he gets in the car. And boy, won't he miss out on a fresh, air-filled pee-fest if he runs away from the opportunity!

Just like Max, we make decisions every day that challenge us to choose between fear and courage. Sure, it might seem safer to stay in your comfort zone and not try something new, but that's not what world-changers are built for. Us world-changers are built to live passionate lives filled with love and purpose. In order to reach the other side, we must be willing to break free from our comfort zone and step out into the playing field, which is where the magic happens.

Follow Your Curiosity

Have you ever wanted to try a sport, learn how to play an instrument, run for student council, join the school newspaper or learn to write computer code, but were nervous about getting started? These fears are completely normal when you are starting out, as the outcome of the situation is uncertain. Whenever I am nervous to try something new, I always remind myself that I will never know the outcome unless I am willing to step outside of my comfort zone and take action.

What's the worst that can happen? This is a question that I ask myself to motivate me to try something new, even if I am not sure I will be good at it. I think that the fear of not being good at something prevents many of us from trying new things. It's all fine and dandy if you make the track team, but on the other hand, it's extremely disappointing to not get chosen.

In Grade Seven, I moved to a new school and decided to try out for the volleyball team. I had played on the junior team at my old school but wasn't exactly a star player. What I didn't realize was that my new school had a very competitive and well-trained team, most of whom played competitively outside of school. I went to all of the tryouts and gave it my best shot, but when the time came to announce the team, my name wasn't on the list. I was devastated. *How embarrassing*, I thought. *Now all of these girls have seen me fail.*

What I didn't realize is that although I hadn't made the team, the coach had another plan for me. "We want you to come to the volleyball camp we host in the summer," he told me. The coach explained that the camp had very skilled trainers who worked with players one-on-one to help improve their technical skills. I could've thrown in the towel at that point and said, *I already got cut from the team, what's the point in trying?* But instead, I chose to pull up my kneepads and give volleyball another try.

That summer I spent a full-week at the volleyball camp learning how to bump, set, spike and serve correctly. I channeled all of my energy into honing my skills and showing the coaches that I really wanted to be on next year's team. I stayed active all summer and got even more volleyball practice during our annual family camping trip in August.

When tryouts came again that fall I was nervous, but ready. Once again I attended all of the tryout dates, gave my best effort and made the team! It was such a great feeling after knowing how hard I had worked to earn this spot. I went on to become a starter for our volleyball team—which made it all the way to the provincial finals. I later made my high school volleyball team and was selected for the regional competitive squad. All of these opportunities came to the girl who got cut from her elementary school volleyball team. And it wasn't because I was some sort of natural volleyball superstar; it was because I was passionate about volleyball and was willing to work hard to be the best player that I could be.

A FAMOUS COMEBACK

In 1978, a 15 year-old boy tried out for his varsity basketball team in North Carolina but was cut because he was shorter than his other teammates.

He moved down to the junior-varsity team and continued to work hard towards his goal of one day playing professional basketball.

This young man went on to become an NBA superstar, widely regarded as the best player in the history of professional basketball.

The boy's name was Michael Jordan.

How I Got My First Job

Sometimes we find our passion and sometimes our passion finds us. All we have to do is be willing to take chances and step outside of our comfort zone to practise leadership and random acts of kindness. As the saying goes: "Opportunity dances with those who are already on the dancefloor."

I was twelve years old when I got my first real job. My mom had taken me to the dollar store after school to pick up a few items. As we were shopping, I noticed a tall, blonde-haired woman with her arms full of goodies. She had lots of party items lodged between her arms and seemed to be concentrating on not dropping anything. My first thought was: *This lady looks like she could use some help.* I walked a few steps towards her and asked, "Excuse me, can I get you a basket?" She turned and looked pleasantly surprised to see a tween girl with braces staring back at her.

"Why yes," she replied in a bemused tone. Nervously, I walked to the front of the store, grabbed a hand basket and brought it to the woman. I held the basket out in front of me, allowing her to easily drop all of her items into the basket without a spill. She took the basket, looked me in the eyes and asked, "Would you like a job?"

I soon learned that the lady was a professional clown who went by the stage name Bubbles. She had been looking to hire new, outgoing clown assistants to help her with children's parties on the weekends. My mom discussed some of the details with Bubbles and arranged my start date. Within a week I learned how to do my own clown face paint and how to make balloon animals—a skill I still proudly make use of today—and officially became Bubbles' assistant, Giggles the Clown!

My dollar store encounter was one example where my passion for working with children and making people laugh found me, but it only found me because I was willing to step out of my comfort zone and offer a random act of leadership. Anybody could have offered that lady a basket—it didn't take any special skill or talent to do so. What it did take was a little bit of courage and the desire to make the world a better place by being the change I wished to see in the world. I had no idea that this seemingly small act of kindness and leadership would lead me to a life-changing job experience. All I knew was that this woman needed help and instead of waiting for someone else to do something, I took it upon myself to be a leader in the situation.

Oftentimes when problems arise, we look to others around us to take action. Sometimes we'll think: *That's not my responsibility*, or, *I don't have the qualifications to handle that situation.* As world-changers, we need to take responsibility for the situations that we face. As the witty story above points out, if everybody waits for someone else to do something, it is quite likely that nothing will get done. And every time we step out of our comfort zone to offer a random act of kindness or leadership we shine our light into the world, which makes it easy for opportunity to find us.

Lessons from Giggles the Clown

I learned a lot about myself during my year working as a professional clown. One of the greatest lessons I took away from my clown days was the importance of not being afraid to make a fool of myself. If you ever want to overcome your fear of standing out, try being a clown for a day! In the clown world your *job* is to stand out. Young children look to you for entertainment. They want to believe that you are real and you have to work hard to earn, and keep, their attention.

As Giggles, I learned to think quickly on my feet. Sometimes Bubbles would hand me the megaphone as we were arriving at a birthday party and tell me to sing Happy Birthday with the puppet as we pulled in the driveway. My twelve year-old self was thinking: *Wait, what? I can't sing! I'm too embarrassed to sing in front of people!* But then I looked out the window at the little birthday girl or boy waiting anxiously for the clown-mobile and I mustered up the courage to sing Happy Birthday.

Other times Bubbles would hand me the "Invisible Dog"—a wire attached to an empty dog collar—and tell me that I needed to stall while she set up for the magic show. Again I thought, *Um, hello, I'm pretty sure these kids are going to realize there isn't a real dog here!* In those moments I had to just go with it and be creative on the fly. When kids would say, "There isn't really a dog there!" I'd respond with a cheeky, "Why, of course there is! You can only see him if you believe." Or when a child would cry after one of my balloon animals popped, I would have to come up with a quick way to ease the situation and stop the crying. Needless to say, clowning kept me on my toes.

All of these lessons helped me build some important skills at a young age. Being Giggles the Clown taught me how to solve problems, improvise, keep calm under pressure and use every resource possible to achieve a desired outcome. And all of this came to be simply because I saw a woman at the dollar store who needed a basket, and I took it upon myself to be the person who offered one to her. The best part about this story is that *anybody* can be the person who offers a basket to someone with their arms full. You don't need any special skills or superpowers, just the willingness to look for ways to help others and the courage to step outside of your comfort zone. It's only when you exit the place of comfort that you can ever find the magic.

Join a Club, or Better yet, Start One!

One of the first questions I ask nearly every young person I meet is, "Are you involved in any clubs or teams at your school?" This is such an important question for me because I am a strong advocate for encouraging extracurricular involvement and volunteerism in young people. You'll never look back on your school experience and say, "Gee, I wish I hadn't been part of all of those clubs and teams." On the contrary, you will almost definitely look back and wish that you had been more involved.

Extracurricular activities were a large part of my life in both elementary school and high school. I *lived* for the group meetings, event planning and team practices that made up my extracurricular calendar. I woke up in the morning feeling excited about the day ahead, mainly because of all of the fun projects and events I had to look forward to.

The pact that I made with my parents was that my marks in school came first. If I maintained honours, I could join as many programs, clubs and teams as I liked. And so, I signed up for every single club, team, group and event that tickled my curiousity, and soon many of these curious endeavours became passions. I loved how I felt after playing on my school soccer team and realized I had a passion for sports and physical fitness. I enjoyed leading meetings at Student Council and learned that I had a passion for event planning. I came alive onstage when emceeing a school event and realized that I had a passion for public speaking. I felt incredibly proud after a poem I wrote was published in the school newspaper and realized that I had a passion for writing.

All of these experiences helped me learn a lot about myself. I learned what I was passionate about, what my best skills were and how to manage all of my commitments in my schedule. Equally important, I learned what I wasn't so passionate about. I tried computer club in Grade Eight where we learned how to type properly (iT nEveR cAughT oN), then I tried chess club to see if I could learn how to think strategically (I never won a game—logic isn't my thing, apparently), and I even tried art club (where I realized that my stick-figure drawings were a little underwhelming). These experiences were invaluable to me, and I look back on them as pivotal development points in my life that shaped me into the person who I am today.

In addition to the personal growth benefits of being involved in my school and community, the extracurricular activities also provided me with a safe space away from the pressures of fitting in. I always felt like a bit of an outsider at school. Not only were some of my physical features and personality traits made fun of, but I also didn't agree with many of the choices my peers were making. I had no interest in partying, drinking alcohol, smoking or doing drugs. I didn't see how any of those things would take me towards my vision of being a world-changer and so I didn't want any part of it. By keeping myself preoccupied with my passions and interests, the social pressures couldn't overtake me and I could continue to focus my energy on building a life of extraordinary leadership.

DISCUSSION QUESTIONS

Chapter Four: Finding Your Passions

1) What vision do you have for yourself when you imagine your future?

2) Why do you think people often find it easier to stay in their comfort zone rather than to take a risk and try something new?

3) What can young people do to take action in finding their passions?

4) The author describes her job as Giggles the Clown as an experience that helped her learn more about her passions. Has there been an experience in your life that helped you discover some of your passions and talents?

5) Are there any clubs/groups/teams at your school that you have thought about joining or starting? What do you think has been holding you back and how can you overcome it?

6) What does your schedule look like after you come home from school? Are you balancing relaxation time with homework and extracurricular activities effectively?

Challenge for the Week

Choose a new hobby/event/activity that you would like to experience and form a plan to make it happen. For example, if you always wanted to try running, do some research, find a race coming up near you and sign-up online to participate—then start training! If you always wanted to learn how to make balloon animals: watch videos online showing you how to get started, purchase a balloon pump and a small bag of balloons and start practising! It doesn't matter what activity you choose; what matters most is that you step out of your comfort zone and try something new.

CHAPTER 5

Leadership as a Lifestyle

"A leader is one who knows the way, goes the way and shows the way."
—John C. Maxwell

When you picture a leader, you might imagine a distinguished-looking individual rallying a crowd of people together for change. This person might be standing on a podium saying dramatic things like, "Hear ye, hear ye!" or, "Now is the time for revolution!" This classic idea of the political-soapbox speaker (at least, it was *my* classic idea) may be charismatic and inspiring, but it is not the only form of leadership.

In early 2015, I conducted a survey through our GIRL TALK Empowerment School Chapters, asking over 600 girls from the Greater Toronto Area about beauty, body image and leadership. One of the survey results that stood out to me was that only 29% of girls see themselves as leaders. That's fewer than three girls out of ten!

Now, what might be the cause of this lack of leaders? I think that the word "leadership" sounds intimidating to many young people. Leadership is commonly associated with business executives and adults—people who are older and who may have earned a management position within their company. This is an outdated idea of leadership that makes becoming a leader seem like a difficult task, reserved for an exclusive class of person. It sounds almost as complex as the process of being knighted by the Queen of England!

The reality is that you don't have to be in a business suit or holding a megaphone to be a leader. Leadership is simply having a vision for the world you'd like to live in, and having the courage to bring your vision to life. I define leadership in terms of two equal roles: **1) Problem Solver:** a person who actively seeks solutions to problems (pretty obvious description, I know); and **2) Peacemaker:** a person who always tries to do what is right instead of what is popular.

Leadership is the heartbeat of what it means to be a world-changer. Changing the world requires vision, courage and commitment, and these are all necessary components of leadership. The time has come for young people to step forward as leaders. This chapter is a practical guide to living a life of leadership. Leading is not just about inspiring speeches or executive management; leading is a choice we make each and every day to be problem solvers and peacemakers.

The World Has Enough Critics

"There isn't enough diversity in the media…all these women look exactly the same!" "Our school has no good teams or groups to be part of." "This field is so dirty…I wish people didn't dump all of their garbage here."

Complaining and criticising are some of the easiest first responses to a problem. Anybody can tell you what is wrong with the world; it's a lot harder to find someone who can tell you what we can do to make it right. Making a complaint about a problem isn't solely a bad thing, so long as it is a first step to you doing something to change it. It's the movement from inaction to action that is required to fix the situation for the better. This is where world-changers come in.

World-changers are solution-oriented. They recognize that identifying problems is easy and that forming solutions takes more effort. If you see a problem, try to find a solution. If you think it's sad that people don't hold open the door for each other anymore, start setting an example by holding open doors for others. If you hate seeing garbage lying around your school property, rally a few people together and start an environmental cleanup committee. There really isn't just one answer for how to solve a problem. The most important part is that you do something—anything—to try to change the situation for the better.

No "Off-Mode" for Leadership

Leadership is not a light switch. It is not something that can be turned on and off when it is convenient. It's not enough to think, "I'm going to go be a leader now at our student council meeting!" as if leadership is a special mode that only comes out in certain circumstances.

No, leadership is a way of being and is a conscious choice that we need to make each and every day. When you commit to being a world-changer you are committing to being a leader. In order to truly live a life of leadership, you need to make the commitment to lead in *all* aspects of your life. Whether you're at school, out at recess, going to the movies, shopping at the mall, on Facebook Messenger with your friends or spending time with your family at home, you need to talk the talk and walk the walk of a leader. World-changing is a full-time job.

I do not mean to suggest that you always have to be perfect. Perfection is an unrealistic and harmful goal no matter who you are. Leadership is not about being perfect. It's about always trying to do what's right. Sometimes your judgment about how to handle a situation might be wrong and you will make a mistake. Making a mistake does not mean that you are no longer a leader. On the contrary, it is often after making mistakes that we have the opportunity to show our true character by doing all we can to right our wrongs. As Martin Luther King Jr. said, "The ultimate measure of a [person] is not where [they] stand in moments of comfort and convenience, but where [they] stand in times of challenge and controversy."

The Importance of Commitment

Once upon a time I tried to skip out on a commitment I had signed up for. I was in Grade Three and had excitedly joined many different clubs and activities at school, including the choir. On one warm spring day, I simply couldn't pass up the opportunity to play wall ball with my male friends instead of going to choir practice. I ran outside with the boys, feeling the exhilaration of rebellion (as rebellious as it ever got for me). And besides, I had memorized all of the choir songs already. Surely, just missing this one time wouldn't hurt.

The object of wall ball is simple: take turns throwing a ball at the wall. If you drop the ball, or fail to hit the wall with your throw, you have to run and touch the wall. The other players then grab the ball and try to throw it against the wall before you reach the wall. If the ball hits the wall before you, you are out.

It's an addictive and competitive game. This particular match seemed to be especially fun—probably because the alternative would have been repetitive choir practice. Whatever the reason, I was a force to be reckoned with at wall ball! I was going to win this game. I could feel it.

Then my mom appeared on the schoolyard.

My heart skipped a beat. I looked over to my left and saw my mother standing outside of the school door with her arms crossed. I could feel all of the blood rush to my face and was immediately embarrassed. I couldn't even work up the courage to turn around and tell the boys to carry on without me. I just stared straight ahead and nervously walked towards her.

"What do you think you're doing?" she demanded, "You're supposed to be at choir practice!"

"I know. It's just..." My excuses sounded lame now that I was trying to verbalize them.

"It is very disrespectful for you to have skipped practice, especially when your teachers have put so much of their own time and efforts into helping put this choir together. Mr. Nepotley has even given you extra training and solo opportunities because he saw your potential, and this is how you repay him?"

I tried to apologize, but she wouldn't hear it.

"I'm not the one who needs the apology. You broke a commitment to your choir instructors and fellow choir members—*they* are the ones who deserve the apology. Come on. You're taking care of this right now!"

My mom took me by the hand and practically dragged me up the school stairs. Some of the kids in the hall were watching us with curious interest. I wanted to cry, but didn't want to make an even bigger scene than the one my mom had already made. My body went numb as we arrived outside of the choir practice room.

My mom knocked on the door. The teacher stopped what he was doing and looked over at us.

"Sorry to interrupt, Mr. Nepotley. Katie has something she would like to say to everyone."

All fifty sets of eyes fell on me. I wanted to float away.

"I...I'm, uhh, I'm s-sorry for missing practice," I managed to stammer out.

There was a pause. Mr. Nepotley seemed to be trying to figure out what exactly had happened. I couldn't bear to tell him where I had been.

"That's alright, Katie," he said, "Come inside, we're happy you're here."

I was relieved that he didn't ask for an explanation in front of everyone. I shuffled into the room and found a seat near the back. My mom quietly shut the classroom door and Mr. Nepotley began conducting once again.

Leaders Are Committed

As humiliating as it was to have to apologize in front of my peers, I am still grateful to my mom for teaching me an important lesson. I had skipped choir for selfish reasons—I didn't feel like going and believed that I already knew everything I needed to know. What I didn't take into consideration is just how much time and energy my choir teacher had been giving to make our performance a success. He didn't *have* to run choir; it was above and beyond his teaching responsibilities. He offered a choir program to give *us* an opportunity to gain experience and learn new musical skills. It was a privilege for me to be in the choir in the first place, and by skipping out I was not only disrespecting myself, but also my teacher who had given up so much of his own time for my benefit.

Now whenever I sign up for a new club, activity or commitment I take my dedication to the group very seriously. I know that when I join a team, their needs become just as important as mine. Imagine it's a Sunday evening and you're scheduled to play a soccer game. It's a cool night and it has started to rain. The last thing you might feel like doing in that moment is playing a cold, wet game of soccer. Pajamas, a couch and snacks sound like a much better option.

But then I think to myself: *What if six players are waiting at the field right now and the team needs just one more player to make the quota to play?* I also try to remind myself that maybe everybody feels the same way as me right now and if we all just decided not to show up, we wouldn't have a team. Leaders take responsibility for their words and actions and understand the importance of commitment. No great accomplishment can be achieved without fully committing to a goal or dream. As leaders we need to be an example for others. We must live in such a way that when we commit to something, we make sure we always follow through to the end without cutting corners.

Words Have Power

World-changers have two main ways to impart change: through their actions and through their words. Actions are usually the primary focus of leadership teachings but it's important to remember that our words are equally powerful. We tend to pick up a lot of the words and phrases we say from our family, friends and the media we consume. Phrases such as "YOLO," "Wazzup," or, "What's the hap?" are fun to say and have become embedded in the North American lexicon. While many of these sayings are light-hearted and innocent, some are harmful. In elementary school, I followed the majority of my peers and began incorporating "That's so retarded" into my vocabulary whenever something was odd or frustrating. Then came all of the wild modifications of this phrase: "You're a tard," or, "What a retard." Around the same time, the phrase, "That's so gay" became popular too. Both of these sayings are still commonplace for many young people (and even some adults!) today.

It wasn't until a guest speaker came to my high school that I recognized that some of the words I had been choosing to use were negative and quite possibly, harmful. The speaker was a young, outgoing girl who shared what it means to be a leader and pointed out that phrases such as "That's retarded" or "That's so gay" are actually very derogatory sayings that have the power to hurt those around us. She explained that when we say these phrases, we are using the words "retarded" and "gay" as synonyms for "stupid," "weird," or "frustrating." I thought to myself, *Oh my goodness; I have been using these hurtful words and didn't even give them a second thought!* It's easy to do when many people around you are saying them too, but it doesn't make it right.

The good news is that we can change our words. The words and phrases that we choose to speak are simply habits that we form over time. If we begin to address the negative words in our life, we can work to clean up our language for the better. The first step in changing our words is paying closer attention to what we say and how we say it. Once I started looking for the moment where "That's so retarded" came to mind, I could make a conscious effort to choose a different phrase. This same methodology applies to other negative uses of language such as swear words or calling people names. We as world-changers need to be aware of the words we choose, since they communicate what kind of people we are and whether or not we walk the walk of being a true leader.

Negative words aren't the only words that have power, however. Positive words are equally powerful in changing the lives of others. Think about the last time someone paid you a sincere compliment. Maybe they told you that you looked really nice or that you are smart or that you speak confidently. How did that compliment make you feel? Probably pretty good. I've had people pay me sincere compliments in the past that meant so much to me that they brightened my whole day. These random words of kindness can be mood-lifters, happiness boosters and day-changers.

The Positive Pushback

Often times, the desire to lead comes from an experience that compels us to change a situation for the better. After all, world-changers are born from the idea that there are problems in the world that need changing.

For me, bullying was one of the main problems that I experienced growing up, so it became the cause that I felt inspired to change from a young age. Not only did I personally experience bullying but I also witnessed many of my peers getting teased. It hurt me to see people being mistreated simply because they were thought to be "weird," "uncool," or "different" from everybody else. This made me angry. So angry that I wanted to do something to change it. And so I did.

The way that I chose to cope with the bullying and challenges I experienced was to take all of the negative energy I felt and redirect it into positive energy. I call this process the Positive Pushback. Instead of fighting problems with hate, I chose to use kindness. Not only are world-changers problem solvers, they are also peacemakers. We seek to find peaceful solutions to some of the most challenging problems.

And so I set up a meeting with my principal to discuss some ideas I had for how I could teach young people about leadership and encourage them to stand up to bullying. I was fortunate enough to have a world-changing principal in high school who took my raw idea and made it even better. Together we ended up creating a one-of-a-kind co-op experience where I had the opportunity to travel to my old elementary school to deliver one-hour workshops to students in Grades Five–Eight over a ten-week period, discussing diversity, self-acceptance and leadership. I kept a record of all the lesson plans I created for the workshops and finished my co-op experience by compiling them into the *Culture of Peace Teacher Resource Manual*—my first official publication. Instead of retaliating against the people who bullied me, I chose to use my personal experiences as a springboard for working with younger students to help encourage them to be leaders and to stand up against bullying.

The Positive Pushback is a very powerful tool for creating change. Instead of feeling defeated by the negative situations that present themselves to you on your journey, use them as motivation to find your passion and take action. Every person experiences trials and challenges; it's how we choose to use them to change the world that separates us as leaders.

Ready, Set, Start!

And so the time has come for you to embrace your calling as a world-changer and to live a life of leadership. Some people say that leaders are born, not made—that the calling to be a leader is only for a select few people. I do not believe this to be true. Although I believe that we all have a unique vocation, I also believe that we all have the opportunity to be world-changers right where we are.

You picked up this book for a reason: likely because you wanted to be a world-changer (or you just found the pink balloon bouquet on the cover mesmerizing!). Perhaps you already see yourself as a world-changer, or perhaps you were looking for the magic secret to world-changing. Either way, I want you to know that you have everything you need to change the world right now. There is no hidden platform or secret sauce or magic bullet. The secret is that there is no secret to being a world-changer! The philosophy of being a world-changer is simple: speak and act in such a way that you make the world around you a better place to be.

If you have a dream, I want you to know that you can achieve it. Do not be afraid of striking out on the first attempt. In order to achieve great things we must be willing to risk our attempts not working out on the first try. If we listen to the naysayers or the voices in our head that tell us we are not good enough how will we ever know what we are capable of achieving?

> Success is not final, failure is not fatal;
> ***it is the courage to continue that counts.***
> *-Winston Churchill*

Oprah Winfrey, one of the most recognizable faces on television, was fired from her job as a television reporter because she was "unfit for television." Walt Disney, the legendary animator, was fired from a newspaper because he "lacked imagination." J.K. Rowling, author of the Harry Potter series, wrote her first book as a struggling single mother on welfare and was rejected twelve times before getting a book deal.

What do all of these people have in common? They took a risk, fell down, and then got back up. Imagine what our world would look like if all of these people had not chosen to step out of their comfort zone and had been too afraid to fail. As leaders, we cannot be afraid of failing. We must be afraid only of not trying. The world isn't going to change itself. The world needs you to change it.

DISCUSSION QUESTIONS

Chapter Five: Leadership as a Lifestyle

1) What does leadership look like to you?

2) Why do you think so few girls see themselves as leaders?

3) Why do you think it's important for leaders to "walk the walk" and "talk the talk?"

4) Have you ever been in a situation where someone skipped out on a commitment? How did it affect you and/or your team?

5) The author describes a Positive Pushback as taking a negative experience and transferring it into positive energy to make a difference. Describe a time in your life where you took a negative situation and turned it into a positive.

6) Can you think of other examples of people besides Oprah Winfrey, Walt Disney and J.K. Rowling who overcame failures and went on to achieve great things?

7) What do you think "leadership as a lifestyle" looks like in action?

Challenge for the Week

Change your language. This week, reflect on some of the words and phrases you use that are negative or hurtful. Make a conscious effort to replace them with world-changing words.

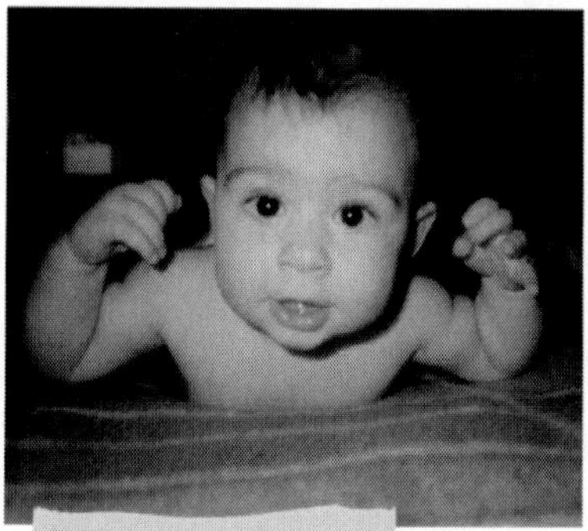

Goal-digging since 1989.

"Giggles" the Clown makes her debut.

My big, crazy, loving family.

Living life on the edge. (Who sits on slides anyhow?)

Me with my granddad at my birthday party.

"Who's that with the camera?" My first real memory of feeling self-conscious about my body.

My groovy, grade 7, blue-haired hippie Halloween costume.

Receiving a trophy at a tournament for my competitive soccer team.

My grade 9 school picture.

The day the esthetician told me I needed to get my eyebrows "done". (A bit blurry, I know, but those brows are clear!)

Being awarded the Governor General's "Caring Canadian" award by the former Governor General, Michaelle Jean.

Cruising through the streets of Oshawa, ON as Miss Fiesta 2009. (That's my dad driving!)

A visual to demonstrate what Duane syndrome looks like. When my eyes are directed to the right (your left), both eyes move to the far side looking towards my right ear. When my eyes are directed to the left (your right), my right eye moves to the far left side but my left eye does not move past the center of my eye, causing a strain, and forcing me to squint slightly.

Me in grade 11 leading a workshop at my former elementary school. My first big gig as a speaker!

Me working hard at my co-op placement at the regional Small Claims Court.

Being awarded the TD Canada Trust Scholarship for "Community Leadership."

Speaking on the TED Worldwide Talent Stage in Vancouver, B.C.

A moment of pride walking on-stage at the 2013 Miss World Canada pageant.

Visiting our GIRL TALK School Chapters in the 2015 School Tour.

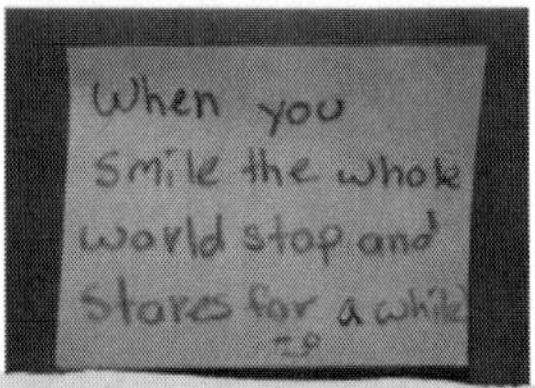

A note from a positive post-it note campaign that a girl in one of our School Chapters became inspired to lead.

Speaking at GIRL TALK Empowerment Day 2015.

The commitment wall at GIRL TALK Empowerment Day 2015. Girls write a personal commitment of how they are going to make their mark in the year ahead.

Some of the messages I hope young people take from my "Dear High School Me" TED Talk (and this book)!

CHAPTER 6

What Your Instagram Profile Says About You

"Don't use social media to impress people; use it to impact people."
—Dave Willis

I'd really like to start this chapter by telling you some important things that your Instagram profile says about you, but first, let me take a selfie…

…just kidding.

Twenty years ago it would have been really strange to carry around a film camera and take pictures of ourselves at every waking moment, then mail all the pictures we took to our friends. These days, cell phones and Instagram make it commonplace. From #iwokeuplikethis bedhead in the morning to #browsonfleek in the evening, our cyber friends and neighbours are seeing more of us than they ever have before—whether they want to or not.

Sure we might see some things we like online (I mean *actually* like, not "Like Button" like) and even hashtag #goals on posts we find inspiring. But are we actually doing anything offline to work towards those goals? At the end of the day, hashtagging something as a #goal doesn't really do anything to bring you closer to achieving it. What's worse, studies show that only supporting a cause or goal online (so-called "Clicktivism") might create a false sense of achievement and prevent you from achieving the goal in real life.

With all of our online connectivity, you might think that young people have unparalleled levels of human communication and togetherness, but this is sadly not the case. Many youth feel more pressure to look and act a certain way than ever before. The Centre for Addiction & Mental Health (CAMH) states that one in five Canadians have a mental health issue, with young people aged 15–24 being most likely to experience mental illness and/or substance abuse disorders than any other age group. Teens and pre-teens are suffering from rising levels of anxiety, stress, depression and even suicide. The total number of 12–19 year olds in Canada at risk for developing depression is a staggering 3.2 million.

Is the fact that mental illness is growing amongst youth as time spent on social media increases, just a coincidence? Many experts don't think so. A study done by Vital Signs Canada found that social networking was listed as the number one most popular group activity for females. The time spent in front of a screen for the average teen is rising as self-esteem falls to an all-time low. This relationship between social media and low self-esteem is unacceptable. We, as world-changers, need to take action.

One thing I don't think we talk about enough is just how much power social media can give us to do bucket loads of goodness—especially when we combine our online posts with offline action! World-changers need to harness this power and use it for social good. In the coming sections I address some of the greatest challenges and pressures young people face online and offer suggestions for how we can rise above and make our mark.

Living Life Outside of a Filter

Not too long ago I found myself looking through some pictures and deciding which one to post for a #throwbackthursday. There was one picture that I thought was a good possible option but the lighting was a little harsh on my face. I was hesitant to post but then thought to myself: *Not to worry, a filter will fix that.*

Wait, what? How strange it was to think that I had the power to freeze a moment and then edit it to make myself and my surroundings appear just as I wanted them to. Too shiny here? Have no fear, we can blotch that out. Taking a selfie in the bathroom mirror? We'll crop out that toilet in no time.

As handy as these instant quick-fix filters and edits may be, they can also give us a false sense of reality. Life doesn't have filters. We can't simply pause moments to edit ourselves before moving forward. If no one told you about the piece of lettuce stuck in your teeth all day, you can't cut it out later—people saw the green menace and there's no turning back now! We need to start loving our imperfect selves and all of our unfiltered quirks, flaws and blemishes.

Sophie Tweed-Simmons, of the TV show *Gene Simmons Family Jewels,* is one celebrity who has made it her mission to change our obsession with filters and instead focus on celebrating the natural. She has dedicated her Instagram page as a #nofilter zone where she only posts unfiltered pictures of herself and her life. In an online world increasingly plagued by Photoshop edits, it is wildly refreshing to see celebrities pushing for a more honest share of life online.

Am I suggesting that you never use the Valencia filter again? No. I personally choose to post a mixture of both filtered and non-filtered photos. What I am suggesting is that we realize that what we post online is really just a *representation* of who we truly are. This reminder becomes especially important when the comparisons begin between others and ourselves.

The Enemy of Comparison

Wow look at how good Stacey looks in that photo; I wish my lips looked as full as hers. Jenna is always travelling to such cool places; I wish I had the money to travel more. Look at how many followers Michelle has; I'll never be as popular as her.

Scroll, scroll, scroll. Compare, compare, compare. Each day we are bombarded by images and stories of other people's lives. This constant viewing of the exciting things everyone else is doing forces us to fall into a comparison trap, where we see the things others (supposedly) have that we wish we had. While these thoughts are seemingly small, they send a powerful message to your psyche. It's almost as if you are repeatedly putting yourself down: *You're not good enough, pretty enough, rich enough or popular enough.*

It's easy to think that everyone else has it all figured out, but the truth is none of us can really live up to our online profiles or carefully crafted photographs. We're all searching to be the ideal girl who has it all together all the time and who looks picture perfect at every moment of the day. The truth is: that girl doesn't exist. It doesn't matter whether you are a superstar or even a supermodel, the Photoshopped version of you will always be an unreachable version of yourself. Top supermodel Cindy Crawford has often felt the pressure to live up to her famous image. As she herself put it, "Even I wish I looked like Cindy Crawford."

When people post on social media they inevitably post their best selves. The selfie that gets posted is of the glowing, million-dollar smile or the fierce, model-inspired duckface. What you don't see are the twenty closed-eyed, awkwardly-posed photos that were immediately deleted. I'd bet that even the so-called "silly pose" photos are pictures where the subject still looks pretty decent. Why are we posting the best versions of ourselves? Because we can. The online world is the one place where we have the power to fully control and perfect our image before advertising it to the world. Some call it vanity and some call it art; perhaps it's a bit of both. What I want you to remember is that what you see others posting about on social media is their highlight reel—the final, edited piece—so don't compare a finished product with your behind-the-scenes moments.

BYOB – Be Your Own Bio

I have the great pleasure of getting to connect with many pre-teen and teenage girls both in person and on social media. I enjoy taking the time to browse many of the girls' profiles on Twitter and Instagram, as I am passionate about encouraging young people to be their best selves and chase their dreams.

One of the trends that I have noticed in viewing these girls' profiles is an increasing fixation on describing one's self in terms of being a follower of a certain celebrity or band. Fan terms such as "Belieber," for followers of Justin Bieber; "Selenator," for devotees of Selena Gomez; and "Directioner," for One Direction fans, have grown to become categories of self-identity. When a young person's bio on social media consists of nothing more than: "Directioner 4 life! <insert band member> is bae," I have to scratch my head.

I mean, sure these performers are great and there's nothing wrong with being a fan, but don't you also want to be more than just a fan? It is sad that in a person's description of themselves, they would dedicate the entire space to talking about someone else. I want you to be your own bio! Tell the world about YOU and how you are changing the world. If we spend all of our time obsessing over the way others are living their life we miss out on the opportunity to live our own lives.

Rating Is Hating

One of my favourite games as a teenager was Monopoly. Or Scrabble. Or Stella-Ella-Ola. While these games are still popular today (except maybe the last one), the social media generation often prefers games such as "Like or Comment for a Rating." In this online "game" a person posts a picture, (often accompanied by the hashtag #bored—see below), and encourages others to "like" their photo so that the picture's poster can then rate the attractiveness of the liker. And yes, the rating is solely based on how hot someone is—or isn't. *Yeesh, I don't remember the Monopoly Man being so critical!*

The main problem with the "Like for a Rating" game is that it reduces people to nothing more than numbers. Referring to someone as a "6" or a "10" completely separates them from you as a real, living person who has thoughts, goals, dreams and yes, feelings. By placing people into a category, we sell them short of their humanity. How does the girl who gets rated a "4" feel when she goes to bed that night? Pretty horrible, I'd imagine. Games should be about *everyone* having fun, not some people having fun at other people's expense. Call me old-fashioned, but I'd like to motion for the "Like for a Rating" game to move away and never return. Let's make a pact to not post pictures that seek a rating or respond to others who post them.

Why You Should Never Be Bored Again

"I'm bored" are two words that should never exist together in a world-changer's vocabulary. When did it suddenly become a cool thing to be bored? The hashtag #bored on Instagram currently has been used over 89 MILLION times! Compare this number with more uplifting hashtags like #inspired (3 million posts), and #motivated (4 million posts). Even combined, these positive hashtags don't come close to the title wave of #bored posts that flood our social media feeds.

Now take a minute to think about the people viewing your #bored posts. What exactly are they supposed to take away from your post? Are they inspired? Encouraged? Empowered? I think not. I've seen many young people post selfies of themselves at home with the hashtag #bored or will post a status like, "Bored. Inbox me." *Wow. Can't wait.*

We as leaders and world-changers should never be bored. There is always so much to be done and lots of inspiration to be spread! The Internet might tell us that it's popular to be #bored, but I think it's far cooler to be #motivated, #encouraged & #inspired. Boredom is passive, complacent and inactive. It isn't going to do anything to change the world. Motivated, inspired and passionate people will.

Cyberbullying Bites

Cyberbullying is bullying that takes place using electronic technology, such as cell phones, computers, and tablets; as well as communication media, like social media sites, text messages, and chat rooms. In 2011, Kids Help Phone published a research update that revealed cyberbullying behaviour is now most rampant on social networking platforms. Texting follows closely as the second most prevalent form of cyberbullying.

CYBER STATS

1 in 5	Canadian teens have witnessed online bullying
25%	of kids between 12-15 have witnessed cyberbullying
51%	of all teens have had a negative experience with social networking
16%	said someone posted an embarrassing photo of them
12%	said someone had hacked their account

Source: Ipsos Reid 2011 Survey of 416 Canadian Teenagers

Cyberbullying really does bite. I've seen far too many young people using social media as a place for hate. From Facebook groups that try to tarnish someone's reputation to negative comments made under posted pictures, these hateful actions can leave lasting scars. Although cyberbullying happens from behind a screen, its effects can be just as harmful as if they were said in person.

The Facebook app "Honesty Box" was really popular during my high school years (it was my generation's version of "Like for a Rating"). Honesty Box allowed people to write anonymous things about you that only you could see. We all secretly hoped that our crush would have the opportunity to tell us that they were in love with us or that we would receive other fantasy-like comments. But I also remember receiving comments like, "You're kinda hot but your voice is annoying." Some of the comments people received in their Honesty Box were far worse and I can imagine how hurtful it would be to read messages of hate sent anonymously.

I also remember seeing just how quickly hate could spread on the Internet when a Facebook group was created that was dedicated to bashing girls who had been nominated for prom queen in my high school. In just one night, publicity of the Facebook group had spread throughout majority of the twelfth graders and led to a heated fight online, continuing the next day at school. People were calling each other names, spreading rumours and gossiping about each other. A few of the targeted girls were heavily bombarded with hateful words and were called many terrible names. Administrators tried to intervene as best as they could, but the bullying continued right up until prom day which made the night unenjoyable for the girls who didn't win prom queen.

As world-changers, we need to be at the forefront of putting an end to bullying in our schools and community. At the end of the day, hate is hate and bullying is bullying. Whether you are spreading rumours, gossip or put-downs, on the Internet or in person, the negative outcomes are the same. When we see someone being bullied we need to choose to take action and say something. Letting someone know that their hateful words or actions are not welcome sends a powerful message—that you will not tolerate hate. Be sure to always report to an authority figure whenever you experience or witness bullying, as they will be able to connect you with resources and step-in when situations are unsafe.

Sexting

Sexting is when people send and receive sexual messages over some form of technology, like a cell phone, web cam, app, or website. Sexts can involve words, videos, or photos. As world-changers we need to be knowledgeable about the risks associated with sexting and ensure that we do our part to keep ourselves—and others—safe.

I felt that it was important to include a section dedicating to sexting because more and more young people are being pressured to send sexts. A 2013 Kids Help Phone survey found that 28% of young people who sent a sext did so because they felt pressured to do so. Girls in particular seem to experience the greatest amount of pressure to post suggestive photos.

If you see someone's image being shared inappropriately it is your responsibility to report to an authority. Any sexting experience that involves blackmail, threats or bullying, could be sexual exploitation and you need to tell someone you trust.

Five Tips For Staying Safe Online

1	Never give out personal information to anyone over the Internet. Period.
2	Be aware that the person who you think you are talking to on the other side of the screen may not necessarily be that person.
3	Do not say anything to anyone over the Internet or through electronic devices that you would not say to them in person.
4	Nothing you do online is truly anonymous. Hate is still hate, bullying is still bullying and messages are traceable.
5	Remember that your online posts, comments, likes and profiles act as a résumé of your character. (Do the "Grandma & Principal Over-My-Shoulder" Test).

The Grandma & Principal Over-My-Shoulder Test

Before posting anything online ask yourself: Would I be comfortable with my grandma or principal standing over my shoulder and watching me post this picture, video or message? Would your grandma feel proud enough to make you cookies after seeing your post? Would your principal give you a gold star of support? If your answer to any of these questions is "no" then perhaps you need to reconsider making the post.

Turning Your Electronics Off

While there are many great benefits to being so interconnected through our phones, laptops, tablets and other electronic devices, there are also equal, if not greater benefits to simply turning off your devices and spending time away from screens.

TAKE A BREAK FROM ELECTRONICS

- ✓ Go for a walk
- ✓ Read a book
- ✓ Have a face-to-face conversation
- ✓ Spend time with your pet
- ✓ Study
- ✓ Make a healthy snack

YOU KNOW YOU NEED A TECH DETOX IF:

- ✗ You text your parents from upstairs in your room asking them to come bring you something
- ✗ You can't go more than ten minutes without checking your phone
- ✗ You'd rather talk to someone online than in person

"I couldn't find my phone charger for a day so I went downstairs to talk to my family. *They seem like nice people.*"

Using Social Media for Social Change

Social media gives us the opportunity to reach people and causes on the other side of the planet with just a click of a button. This is exciting because it means that we can use our profiles and followings to spread ideas that matter. Whether you have ten followers or ten thousand followers, all it takes is one great post to rally others around your cause.

It's now possible for anyone to start a campaign or project and mobilize people locally and/or across the world to make a change. Imagine how challenging it must have been decades ago when the only way to share about your ideas was in person. Don't get me wrong, face-to-face conversations have incredible power to build your platform and are an essential part of championing a cause. However, in the time it takes me to approach one person face-to-face, I can easily make a single post on social media and reach hundreds, possibly thousands, of people. This new technology is a form of power and we need to use it wisely.

There are many ways to be a world-changer online: signing petitions, sharing inspiring stories, sharing your opinion on issues you are passionate about, and more. Even simple boosts of encouragement to your friends or paying someone a compliment online has the power to make someone's day a little brighter and make the world a little bit better.

WORLD-CHANGING HASHTAGS

#firstworldsolutions
#inspiringwomen
#GIRLTALKBook
#GIRLTALKDay
#worldchanger
#bethechange
#motivation
#inspiration
#HeforShe

World-Changing Websites

GirlTalkEmpowerment.com
Our #FirstWorldSolutions page has dozens of shareable images with inspiring stats and quotes that are easy to share on your Facebook, Twitter or Instagram page. We also have a Tumblr linked to our website with weekly blogs related to all things empowerment. We're constantly updating new ideas and events, so be sure to keep checking in!

Change.org
The world's largest online petition platform, empowering people everywhere to create the change they want to see. The site makes it easy to sign petitions for causes that you care about or even to create your own petition! Popular topics range from human rights, education, the environment, animals and criminal justice—just to name a few. It doesn't matter whether your cause is local or global; there is a place for you on this site. You can then share your petition on your social media sites to rally signatures and get your cause noticed in a big way.

UN.org
The United Nations is an international organization composed of 193 countries from around the globe, which work together to take action on the issues confronting humanity in the 21st century. These issues include: climate change, human rights, gender equality, food production, and more. Their website includes links to news, media and current world issues as well as volunteer opportunities. You can also follow their many sub-organizations and campaigns on social media such as the #HeforShe campaign, which encourages boys to take a stance against gender inequality. Actress Emma Watson is the lead spokesperson of the #HeforShe campaign.

DISCUSSION QUESTIONS

Chapter Six: What Your Instagram Profile Says About You

1) Why do you think depression, anxiety and other mental illnesses are on the rise for young people?

2) How have Photoshopped and filtered pictures changed the standard of beauty for girls and women? How can we change this new standard?

3) How do you feel after learning that even top supermodel, Cindy Crawford, says she wishes she looked like the Photoshopped version of herself?

4) Why do you think #bored posts are so popular?

5) What can be done to address cyberbullying when you see it?

6) What are some ways that you can use social media for social change?

Challenge for the Week

Take time to write a short bio—no more than one hundred and fifty characters—all about you. This is your time to brag: focus on your passions, interests and accomplishments in a fun and creative manner. Once you're happy with your final piece, make this description your new bio on Instagram/Twitter or any other social media profiles. (We'd love to see a #Worldchanger and/or #GoalDigger hashtag in there!)

CHAPTER 7

Taking Care of You

"Take care of your body; it's the only place you have to live."
—Jim Rohn

Imagine for a moment that you are the owner of a beautiful, prize-winning racehorse. Your horse is a disciplined athlete that needs to train several times a week in order to prepare for its competitions and events. Your horse requires daily care and maintenance to perform at its highest level. If it trains too hard on one day, it will likely need to take time the next day to rest. If it gets sick, it will need extra nurturing to get it back to its healthy state. The success of the horse lies not only in how hard it trains but also in how it is taken care of. The horse will not be able to perform to its best ability if it is under-trained, over-trained, stressed or overworked. The key to success is all about balance, ensuring that the horse has all of the tools it needs to perform at optimal level.

Like racehorses, world-changers need to live a life of balance. Being a world-changer is no easy feat—it's a lifelong commitment that will be filled with lots of ups, downs and zigzags. We need to ensure that we prepare ourselves for the full lives we lead. How can we expect to have the energy to follow our passions if we are always tired and sleep-deprived? How can we expect to set goals for ourselves if we are always bogged down by stress? How can we expect to love others if we don't first love ourselves?

This chapter is dedicated to providing you with ideas and inspiration on how to make time for yourself so that you have all of the tools you need to change the world. From nutrition, to stress-management, to fun fitness ideas, my goal is to encourage you to take charge of your health so that you have the energy to chase all of your dreams.

But First, YOU

Yes, you. You are your most valuable resource. In your quest to make your mark on the world, challenges are bound to arise and obstacles that you hadn't considered before will appear along the way. There may be days when you feel alone and find that some people do not understand your vision. In order to be prepared for the journey that lies ahead you need to ensure that you equip yourself with a healthy mind, body and spirit. This process of taking care of yourself is also known as practising self-love.

Self-love is defined as "regard for one's own wellbeing and happiness." World-changing truly starts from within. How we care for our minds, bodies and souls directly impacts how we feel about ourselves and the world around us. Self-love includes many diverse aspects, such as choosing nourishing food, taking time for exercise, pausing for moments of reflection and living a life filled with balance. Below is a list of self-love inspirations that I hope will serve as feel-good encouragements for you to reflect on and look back to as you move forward on your path.

10 Self-Love Inspirations for World-Changers:

1	Speak from the heart.
2	Be kind to yourself and to others.
3	Don't be afraid to say "no."
4	Don't be afraid to say "yes."
5	Let go of what brings you down.
6	Surround yourself with people who lift you higher.
7	If it feels wrong, it probably is.
8	Forgive yourself when you make a mistake.
9	Live for the moments you won't forget.
10	Believe that you have it all because the truth is you already do.

You Are Worth More than the Numbers on the Scale

Girls and scales have long been at war. A survey of 300 women of all sizes by Glamour Magazine in 2011 found that on average, women have 13 negative body thoughts daily—nearly one for every waking hour. Ninety seven percent of women experienced at least one "I hate my body" moment per day and some women even admitted to having 35, 50 or 100 negative body thoughts in a twenty-four hour period. And what tends to be the largest negative critique? Their weight. Whether it's feeling too skinny or too fat, it seems that we girls struggle to love our bodies because of the numbers on the scale.

I was always one of the tallest girls in my elementary school class, and with my extra height came extra weight. I would hear girls talking about their weight in the changeroom before gym class, and I started to become self-conscious when I didn't hear anybody saying that they weighed over 100 pounds—which I did. Whenever any of the girls asked me about my weight, I would awkwardly dodge the question. It wasn't long before I started feeling uncomfortable about my weight and body shape. Like many girls, I began looking in the mirror and having "I hate my body" moments from time-to-time.

The "I hate my body" thoughts take bites out of our self-confidence, often with long-lasting effects. What I wish I had known in Grade Six is that there isn't one magical size or weight that equals good health. We are all different shapes and sizes and each body type has a different healthy weight. Size two, although healthy for some body types, is not the only dress size that equals good health. And just because you are a size two doesn't mean that you are healthy. It is important to see a doctor regularly for checkups with at least one physical examination each year. The doctor will measure your height, weight, blood pressure and other metrics, and provide charts to show whether or not you are in the healthy weight range for your age and height.

Above all, it is always important to remember that your worth is not determined by any dress size or weight number. Your worth, purpose and value goes far beyond any number on a scale. We are not finished products; we are constantly changing and evolving. Choosing to take care of your health is not just about how you look, but how you feel.

There have been times in my life when I fell into unhealthy, junk food-filled eating habits. Meals consisting of fries, soda and doughnuts—just to name a few items—are one-way tickets to feeling sluggish and tired. A 2009 study conducted by The Journal of the Federation of American Societies for Experimental Biology found that some of the effects of high fat/high sugar/high salt diets include poor concentration, mood problems, poor sleep and poor exercise capabilities. Talk about motivation killers for world-changers! We need to remove ourselves from only focusing on how food affects our appearance and instead focus on how the foods we choose to eat make us feel.

Food Is Our Fuel

Cars need gasoline in order to run. Humans need water and food in order to live. The foods and drinks we choose to put into our bodies supply us with the nutrients we need to support all of our bodily functions and day-to-day living. We need to see the food that we eat as fuel for our body and remember that if we want to look and feel our best, we are going to need to fill ourselves with nutritious foods.

There is a common misconception that eating healthy means eating less. It is this misconception that causes thousands of girls to start unhealthy diets that usually involve limited calories and starvation. When I talk about my own "diet," I use it in the traditional sense—namely, the types of food I eat on a daily basis. Unfortunately our society has taken the word "diet" to mean starving the body or cutting out certain food groups. A study conducted by the Canadian Women's Foundation found that 50% of Grade Six girls are unhealthily dieting, and by Grade Ten this number increases to 60%. These statistics are scary because many diets give false information about what is truly healthy for your body.

The next time you think about healthy eating don't just think about what you need to subtract from your diet; think about what you need to add to ensure that you are meeting all of the food groups. Health Canada has created a practical guide to eating well to help make it easier to understand all of the different foods that should be included in your diet. For more info visit: healthycanadians.gc.ca.

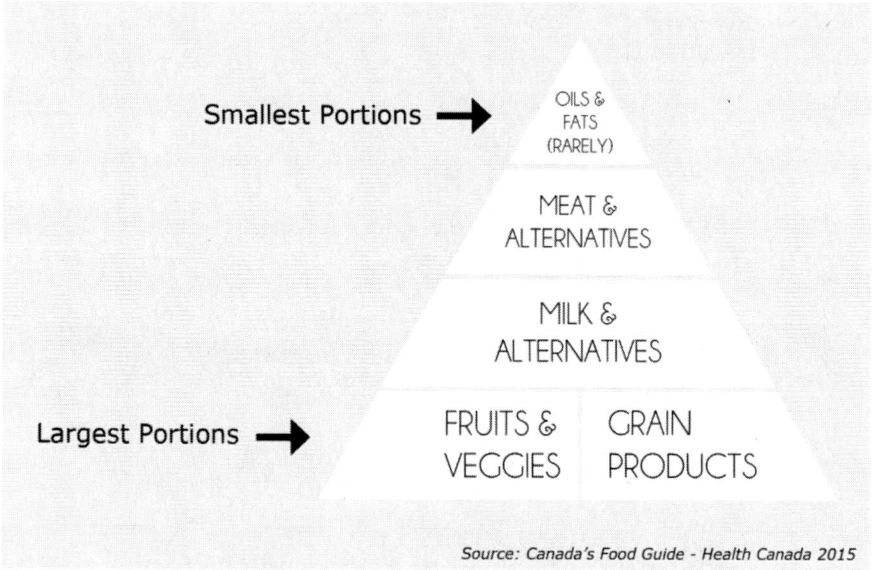

What is meant by "junk food?" Junk food is typically defined as foods with little nutritional value that are high in calories, fat, sugar or salt. Common examples of junk food include chips, cookies, sodas, ice cream, fries and candy. The main problem with junk food is that eating it triggers the brain to want even more food. According to the UK Telegraph, these triggers can last for several days and cause you to overeat. So not only is the original junk food serving lacking nutrients—and no, ketchup does not count as a vegetable serving—it also sends your brain into a state where it wants even more junk food! This is the negative cycle that is important for us world-changers to break free from. Sure we can treat ourselves every once in a while, at special events or nights out with friends, but that should only be about 10% of the time. The other 90% of our day-to-day living should be filled with nutritious and delicious whole foods to keep us energized and well-nourished.

Did You Know?

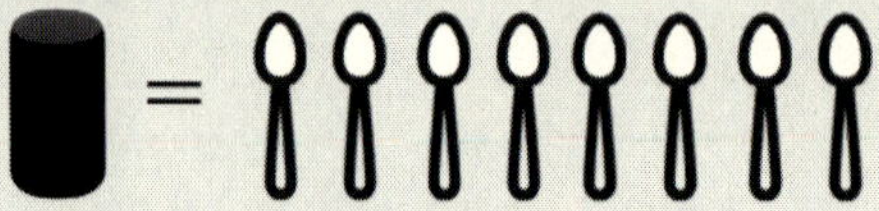

A can of Coke contains 35 grams of sugar
(that's just over 8 teaspoons!)

If you have a Big Mac, fries and a Coke, you'd need to walk for nearly six hours straight just to burn off those calories.

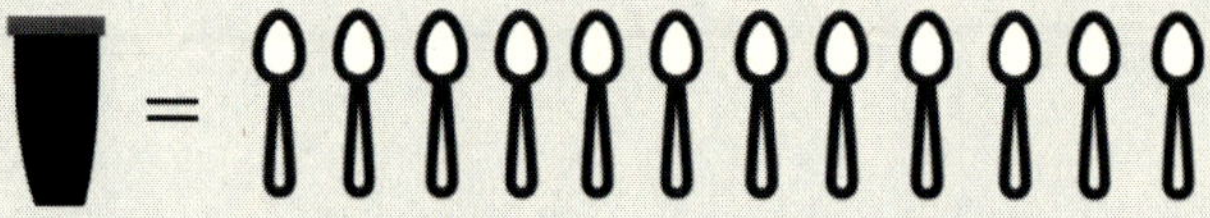

A Grande Pumpkin Spice Latte at Starbucks does not actually have any pumpkin in its ingredients and contains 49 grams of sugar (nearly 12 teaspoons!)

Healthy Food Swaps:

Instead of...	**Try this!**
Breakfast cereal	Oatmeal with berries
White bread	Whole grain bread
Processed peanut butter	Natural almond butter *(Nothing but almonds!)*
Potato chips	Stovetop popcorn
Dried fruits	Fresh fruits
Sweetened latte	Herbal tea
Sodas, juices & energy drinks	Water *(Add lemons & limes for extra flavour!)*

Quick & Healthy Snack Ideas:

- ✓ Apple slices served with a spoonful of natural almond butter
- ✓ Vegetables with hummus or salsa as a dip
- ✓ Unsweetened yogurt with fresh berries on-top
- ✓ A handful of mixed, unsalted nuts
- ✓ The Four-Ingredient Cookie *(See recipe below)*.

The Four-Ingredient Cookie Recipe

These cookies are so easy to make and are one of my favourite go-to snacks. I love a good cookie and having this healthy option in the house gives me the sweet taste I crave while fueling my body with feel-good ingredients.

FOUR-INGREDIENT COOKIES

Ingredients:

1 cup of rolled oats
2 bananas
1 heaping spoonful of natural almond butter
1/3 cup of dark chocolate chips

Instructions:

1. Preheat the oven to 350 degrees Fahrenheit.*
2. In a mixing bowl mash up the peeled bananas using a potato masher or fork until the bananas are a soft, squishy consistency.
3. Add oats, almond butter and dark chocolate chips to the mashed banana and mix well.
4. Drop bite-sized spoonfuls of the mixture onto a parchment-lined baking sheet and bake for 12-15 minutes.

**Be sure to seek help from a parent or guardian if this is your first time baking.*

A Little Fitspiration

Healthy is the new skinny. Instead of striving for a goal weight or dress size we should strive for optimum health. A large component of living a healthy life is physical fitness. Packed with mega health benefits, staying active can have a huge impact on your quality of life. A study conducted by the British Columbia Centre of Excellence for Women's Health in 2013 found that "physical activity has a positive effect on mood, cognitive functioning, psychological well-being, and negative mood associated with pre-menstrual syndrome (PMS), and has been shown to decrease levels of anxiety, depression, and psychological stress." They also found that physical activity for girls is particularly important in the development of a positive self-concept and contributes to general health and well-being.

Exercise has played an important role in my life. When I was going through tough times in school, exercise helped boost my mood and keep me focused on my goals. To this day I still look and feel my best when I work out. I love feeling strong and seeing myself achieve new fitness goals like being able to do more than one pushup and running longer distances.

Fitness should be part of your everyday routine. Health experts recommend that you get thirty minutes of exercise a day. This doesn't have to be thirty minutes all at once—it can be split into smaller intervals. So how can you fit exercise into your day? Make time! There are many different ways to get exercise and so it's important that you pick methods that make you feel good. Talking to your family about signing you up for a gym membership and/or sports team is one way to add in extra exercise. Some of these memberships can be expensive, which is why you can also try out for school teams and join intramurals to enjoy low-cost fitness benefits. But beyond all of these things, there are also very simple ways to add fitness into your everyday life. If you start making some of these practices a regular part of your day, they will eventually become habits that will prepare you for living a healthy lifestyle.

Easy ways to add more movement into your day:

- ✔ Skip the elevator and take the stairs
- ✔ Make walking the dog (or guinea pig) part of your daily after-school routine
- ✔ During your lunch hour take time to go for a walk around the school after you have finished eating
- ✔ Walk or ride your bike to school
- ✔ Put your headphones in at home and dance to some of your favourite tunes
- ✔ If you're watching TV, try to stand up and walk around during commercial breaks (maybe even do 10 jumping jacks?)
- ✔ Walk around your room while you are talking on the phone
- ✔ Offer to help carry-in groceries

Stress Less

When you've got an exam on Thursday, a soccer tournament on Saturday, work on Sunday morning, a friend's surprise party you're organizing on Sunday night and an essay due Monday, life can be a bit stressful. As world-changers, our schedules are frequently full as we make time for school, work, family, friends and our passions. It is possible to manage all of our interests if we first learn how to manage our stress.

One of the best ways to manage stress is to keep an organized agenda. In high school I began regularly using a personal agenda book to organize my life. I started by taking the course overviews that I received in the first week of school and plugging all key dates into my agenda (e.g. Thursday, October 11: Geometry Test). I would then mark down any practices, meetings or other important events that I could plan in advance (e.g. "Band Practice, 4–6pm" every Wednesday or "Student Council meeting February 9 at lunch"). The process of writing all important dates into my agenda immediately makes me feel more organized. Once I can see my schedule laid out I can better plan my life and ensure that I can keep all of my commitments. I can also see in advance if I am going to have any conflicts, like if a teacher schedules a test the same day as a cross-country meet. If this happens, I would always approach the teacher to explain the conflict and see if an alternate test date could be made for me. It's very important to keep open communication with your teachers and coaches so that you can balance your schedule and make arrangements to fit all of your commitments in.

Another handy tool that accompanies agenda-keeping is making to-do lists. I draw little empty squares beside each of the to-dos in my lists so that I can check them off as I complete them. I get exceptionally excited when I get to check off something on my list, as it feels like a great achievement each time I complete an important task.

Managing stress is an ongoing process. Even with solid agendas and to-do lists there will always be unforeseen challenges that come our way and cause us stress. Although managing stress is part of being a good student, employee or world-changer, it's also important that we take time to simply relax and de-stress. If you feel overwhelmed be sure to step away from your tasks and make time for fun. Below is a list of some great stress-busting activities to help get you back to a better state of mind.

Stress-busting Activities:

- Start a journal
- Go for a walk
- Make a vision board
- Listen to music
- Take a warm bath or shower
- Spend time with your pet

When You Are Having a Bad Day

There are days where even the most confident people feel down. Not every day is going to be wonderful, and there will be some days where the pressures pile up and feel like too much to handle. In these moments the most important thing to do is to talk to someone you trust. This book is called *GIRL TALK* because that is exactly what I would like girls to do: talk, share, discuss and brainstorm. As fellow female empowerment leader and three-time Amnesty International award winner, Sally Armstrong says, "We all know that if you can't talk about something you can't change it."

If you are going through a really tough time make sure that you talk to someone and ask for help. You are not alone and no matter what challenge you face, something can be done to protect you and keep you safe. Talk to a parent, guardian, aunt, sister, grandmother, teacher, coach or neighbor—whoever you feel closest to. The worst thing you can do in a dark moment is to keep everything bottled up inside. HelpGuide.org, an online source for mental health resources, states "talking about your stress with a calm and balanced listener will make you feel better instantly." After all, if nobody knows what you're going through, they won't be able to help get you the advice or assistance you need.

childhelplineinternational.org is a global network available for young people that will help connect you to an organization specializing in counselling.

*THIS WEBSITE LISTS CONTACTS IN **145** DIFFERENT COUNTRIES*

In Canada we have the **Kids Help Phone**, a toll-free, 24 hour, national bilingual telephone counselling service for children and youth. This service offers online and phone counselling, as well as information on young people's issues and interactive activities.

*CONNECT WITH THEM AT **KIDSHELPPHONE.CA** OR **1-800-668-6868***

A World-Changing Self-Love Mantra:

There is nobody else just like me. I have unique gifts and talents to offer the world. I may not be the best at everything but I will always try my best. If I fall down, I will push myself back up. I know that wherever I go I am not alone, and that if I am overwhelmed I can always ask for help. Today I choose to be me. I believe I can do anything I put my mind to and that the best is yet to come. I am thankful for all of my blessings and will use my time to spread love and kindness. I know that I have a purpose and that with my words, actions, dreams and goals; I can make my mark on the world.

DISCUSSION QUESTIONS

Chapter Seven: Taking Care of You

1) How do you currently practise self-love in your day-to-day routine?

2) Which of the 10 Self-Love Inspirations is your favourite? Why does it speak to you the most?

3) Why do you think girls and women have so many "I hate my body moments" in a day? How can we change this?

4) Which of the "Did You Know?" food facts surprised you the most? Will this change how you look at fast food?

5) Which of the Healthy Food Swaps can you add to your diet?

6) How many times a week do you exercise? What are some new ways that you can add fitness to your daily routine?

7) How do you cope with stress? Who do you talk to when you are having a bad day?

8) What are some positive habits you could add to your daily routine to help bring you closer to your goals?

Challenge for the Week

Choose a positive habit that you would like to incorporate into your daily routine and be sure to make time for it each day of the week. Ideas: flossing once a day, drinking 6–8 glasses of water a day, turning off social media after 7:00 p.m. etc. Who knows, you might like your new habit so much it becomes part of your everyday routine!

CHAPTER 8

The Company You Keep

"Only surround yourself with people who will lift you higher."
—Oprah Winfrey

A tree grows tall towards the sky, yet stays grounded because of its roots. Like trees, all world-changers need a strong support system to nurture their spirit as they reach for their dreams. The company we keep has a great influence on how we live our lives. These are the people who are with us during our highest and lowest moments and who experience the day-to-day intricacies of life with us. They see us at our best and they see us at our worst. We learn from them and they learn from us. They're our very own tribe and we need to choose them carefully.

World-changers thrive best when they are surrounded by other world-changers. You need to surround yourself with people who are like-minded. They don't have to have the same interests or hobbies as you, but they should have the same values. Traits such as optimism, honesty, compassion and loyalty are all highly attractive and compatible qualities for world-changers. These are the types of inspiring traits that will lift you up and re-energize you on even the toughest days. After all, we can't choose the challenges that come our way in life, but we can choose the people we want to have on our team for the journey.

Attitude Is Contagious

The company we keep has a significant influence on our mood, perspective and mindset. If we spend our time with people who complain and criticize frequently, there is a good chance that these traits will eventually start to rub off on us. Once one apple in a basket starts to turn bad, its mould spreads to the other apples. Soon enough the entire basket is mouldy. Apples that were once tasty and fresh can quickly turn into a stomach-turning, decomposing mess, all because they were in contact with one bad apple.

Similarly, world-changers can be influenced by those with whom they are in close proximity. On several occasions I have found myself in uncomfortable situations where classmates, teammates, friends, co-workers or even strangers have included me in conversations I wanted no part of. *"I'm going to get soooo drunk tonight." "Did you see how frumpy Kaitlyn looks in those pants?" "I hate my job, so basically I just stay on Facebook all day and nobody even cares."* These are all conversation pieces that take a serious toll on my inspiration meter. After being involved in these kinds of conversations, I find that I need a lengthy recovery time to get back to my normal, upbeat self.

Have you ever had an experience where you walked away from a conversation feeling drained of energy? This is not the type of feeling we want to have with the people we choose to keep in our inner circle. For the most part, the conversations that we have should lift us up, whether we are sharing about a current project we're working on or asking someone else how their day is going.

I do not mean to suggest that every conversation you have should be all giggles and cheer. Of course, there will be times when your discussions will be more sombre—if you had a bad day, if the person you're talking to had a bad day, if you're disappointed about something etc. World-changers are allowed to have crummy days and crummy conversations sometimes. The point I am making here is that if most of your conversations with friends leave you feeling down and drained, it might be a sign that you need to reevaluate who you keep in your inner circle.

Your Inner Circle

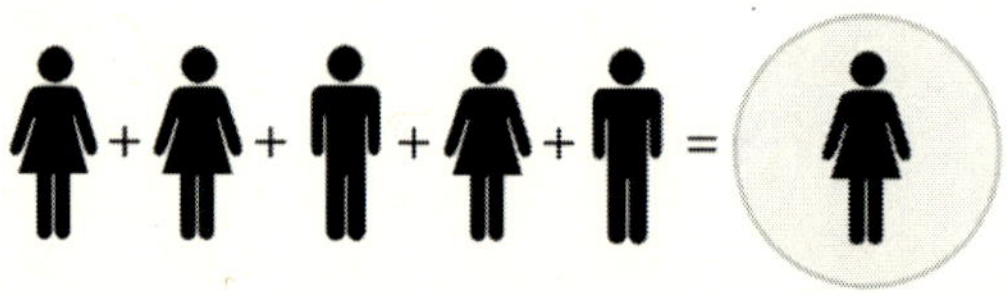

"You are the average of the five people you spend the most time with."
—Jim Rohn

I want you to take a moment and make a list of who the five people are in your life that you spend the most time with:

1) ______________________________

2) ______________________________

3) ______________________________

4) ______________________________

5) ______________________________

Take a look at the list you have created. How do you feel when you spend time with each of these people? Are the people you spend time with passionate about changing the world like you? What do you typically talk about when you spend time with these people? Do they support your vision? Look for patterns and personality traits amongst your list. Is there anyone on your list that could be considered a bad apple?

As world-changers, it is important for us to dedicate as much time and energy as possible to the things that fuel our soul and vision. If we're truly going to make a difference in the world, we need to ensure that we build an environment of support around us to congratulate us on the good days and give us boosts of encouragement on the bad days. What we don't need in our inner circle are doubters or critics pushing us away from our goals and dreams.

People, Events & Ideas

Eleanor Roosevelt, an inspiring American politician and activist, once said, "Great minds discuss ideas; average minds discuss events; small minds discuss people." Powerful words from a lady who certainly knew a thing or two about dreaming big. Eleanor was a true world-changer in her role as First Lady of the United States and beyond. Not only did she serve on the United Nations Human Rights Commission, but she also oversaw the drafting of the Universal Declaration of Human Rights and was an advocate for the rights of women and minorities.

Eleanor Roosevelt was a world-changer who realized the importance of having a like-minded inner circle. The friends you keep, and the things you talk about, will say a lot about you as a person and a leader. Below is a summary of each of the subjects mentioned in Eleanor's quote, and how they relate to the discussions you have with your inner circle:

1) **People**: Talking about other people is what Eleanor referred to as the "small-minded" category. This category focuses on comparison—not empowerment. Gossip, rumours and criticisms would all qualify as part of a discussion about people. Trying to put others down does not lift us up. In fact,

it almost works in reverse. As the saying goes, "What Sally says of Suzie says more about Sally than it does of Suzie."

2) **Events**: Event discussion could include things like talking about what you did on the weekend or when the next party is coming up. Events focus on what is—not on what could be. Although there is nothing wrong with looking forward to the release of the next movie blockbuster or enjoying social nights, these topics do not do anything to move your own ideas forward. So keep these discussions in-check and make sure that they don't consume all of your conversation time.

3) **Ideas**: Talking about ideas is what Eleanor associated with "great minds." Ideas are a combination of our curiosities and passions coming together to form new thoughts. Ideas are the beginning of every great dream or goal and the heartbeat behind a vision. Without ideas there would be no world change.

It's important to note that talking about events and people do not always have to be negative. Rather, anytime that you have a chance to talk about either of these subjects you should try to focus on the positives. Talk about people whom you admire, or about world-changing events that you are looking forward to being part of. Finding the positive side of every situation is part of the DNA of being a world-changer. We can use our influence to start conversations that matter and encourage others to think big.

World-changers obsess about ideas, everything from possible new inventions to how best to tackle a current global challenge. We delight in the possibility that each new day brings, and celebrate each victory along the way. When we see a headline about changes happening to the environment, we begin brainstorming ways that we can help make an impact. When we hear that it is Bullying Awareness Week coming up soon, we bring ideas back to our school clubs of how we can host an anti-bullying campaign. World-changers also lift up other world-changers and their great ideas. Ideas are what keep us up at night thinking what our next great project is going to be, and they wake us up in the morning with an inspired passion to do something great.

Tongue-Tied

We all have moments where our emotions get the best of us and we say something that we don't mean to say. Perhaps you get into a fight with someone and they call you a name and then you respond back with another name. On the best of days you wouldn't have even thought to name-call but somehow it came out in the moment of anger.

I remember hearing a police officer speaking to a group of youth a few years back, giving lessons on mistakes: "If you make a mistake, put your hand up. Confess to what it is you have done, apologize, and move forward." This is solid advice for any world-changer. We *all* make mistakes, but the true measure of a person's integrity is how they choose to fix their mistakes and make things right.

Mistakes have a way of lingering on my conscience for some time. It's hard knowing that something was your fault and that it has caused hurt to someone else. In these moments I remind myself that my intention hadn't been to cause any harm and therefore I cannot be too hard on myself. I also make a decision to do everything in my power to make the situation right. Calling the person to apologize, sending a note, surprising them with flowers or even initiating an honest face-to-face discussion are all great ways to help make a negative situation a positive one.

Mother Teresa said, "Let no one ever come to you without leaving better and happier. Be the living expression of God's kindness: kindness in your face, kindness in your eyes, kindness in your smile." I think this is a good philosophy for world-changers to live by. If we truly want to change the world, we have to change *our* world. This means building up the people around us so that they feel empowered to change their world too.

Dating Notes from a Blue-Haired Hippy

Two days before our Grade Seven Halloween Dance, one of the boys in my class (whom I had a crush on) asked me if I would save him a dance. Me being the bashful, slightly-awkward pre-teen that I was, I could not imagine that he would pick me out of all the girls in my class. "Are you just going around asking everybody?" I asked sheepishly. The boy left pretty quickly after that, most likely feeling confused (poor guy). But I felt giddy and was even more excited about getting my costume together for the school dance so I could have a magical dance with my crush.

The morning of the dance came and I jumped out of bed with excitement, ready to get my costume on. My mom had helped me put together a nifty hippy costume complete with a blue wig, bell-bottom jeans and a large sign that read, "Freedom Is Peace." Boy, was I ready for this dance to get started!

Apparently, I was one of the only ones ready for the Halloween Dance. It was quite a shock walking into the gymnasium to find only about nine other kids (out of 50) wearing a full costume. There I was, standing with all of the noncostumed girls on one side of the gym, waiting for my crush—or any boy for that matter—to come and dance with me. But sadly, he never came.

Perhaps I had confused him with my nervous response a few days before or maybe it was my loud and proud hippy costume that turned him away. Whatever the reason, I made a vow that I would never change myself just to fit in or to have a boyfriend. Heck, if nobody wants to dance with me dressed as a hippy, then they don't get to dance with me at all! (And they also won't get to share in on the sweet prize I won for best costume—hello mall gift card!)

And so the dating world never became a main focus of my attention even as I moved into high school. I decided that I was going to keep focusing on my goals and that the right fellow world-changer would come along when it was meant to happen. I didn't just want a relationship to fit in; I wanted to wait for my partner-in-shine (partners-in-crime are so last decade!). In my opinion, the best relationships occur when two mature and confident individuals come together to change the world. In elementary and high school, everybody is still trying to figure themselves out. It is rare to find someone at that age that will be fully committed to you and secure enough to encourage you to continue world-changing. I witnessed too many friends and peers fall into the *I-want-to-have-a-boyfriend-so-bad-I-will-do-anything-to-have-one* trap where they would start desperately looking for a boyfriend just so they could have someone's hand to hold at lunch. There is a big difference between dating someone because you just want to have a boyfriend and dating someone because you want to change the world with them.

Although I didn't find my partner-in-shine until after high school, you may be one of the rare people who do happen to find a world-changing partner-in-shine in your teen years. So if you choose to date in high school or beyond, make sure that you are dating for the right reasons (a.k.a. this person sparks a world-changing light within you) and don't settle for any treatment less than what you deserve.

Healthy Relationships

Even the best relationships have their challenges. There are times in every relationship where you will have a disagreement and sometimes those disagreements can lead to people getting their feelings hurt. Disagreements are a natural part of any relationship and as long as the arguments are respectful, the disagreement is healthy. A relationship becomes unhealthy when a pattern of repeated, disrespectful words and actions occur.

Although most girls seek comfort from their families when they are going through difficult times, many also experience some of the unhealthiest relationships in their own homes. Broken marriages, illness, addictions, financial stress, violence, depression and other challenges that our families experience have a profound impact on our upbringing. The emotions and stresses of our families naturally fall on our shoulders and affect our mood.

It's important that we remember that no person or family is perfect. Everybody makes mistakes and we all have obstacles to overcome in our life. Even if we come from some of the darkest circumstances, it doesn't do us any good to blame all of our problems on our family members. We need to practise forgiveness.

Forgiveness is the process of removing resentful feelings toward someone for an offense, flaw or mistake. When you forgive someone it releases you from the overwhelming burden of hate and allows you to spend your time and energy living in the present.

How you should feel in a HEALTHY Relationship	How you might feel in an UNHEALTHY Relationship
Respected	Disrespected
Empowered	Powerless
Protected	Unsafe
Trusted	Betrayed
Valued	Ignored
Accepted	Ashamed
Comforted	Overwhelmed
Hopeful	Depressed

If you feel that one or more of the relationships in your life have traits that fall in the Unhealthy Relationship category above, you need to speak to someone you trust. Talk to a family member, friend, teacher, coach or neighbour who makes you feel safe and let them know what you are going through. If you don't have someone close to you who you can trust, or if you want an outside opinion, try contacting a third-party organization as mentioned in the previous chapter. In Canada, you can call the Kids Help Phone 24 hour service at 1-800-668-6868. Youth internationally can visit the Child Help Line website (www.childhelplineinternational.org) to find the closest phone help line to them.

Say "Thank You"

When was the last time you grabbed your mom and gave her a hug to thank her for everything she has done for you? Did you ever tell the math teacher who always encouraged you just how much her kindness meant? Life is short and moments are fleeting. When you get the opportunity to tell someone that you love them or that you are thankful for what they have done, you should always take it.

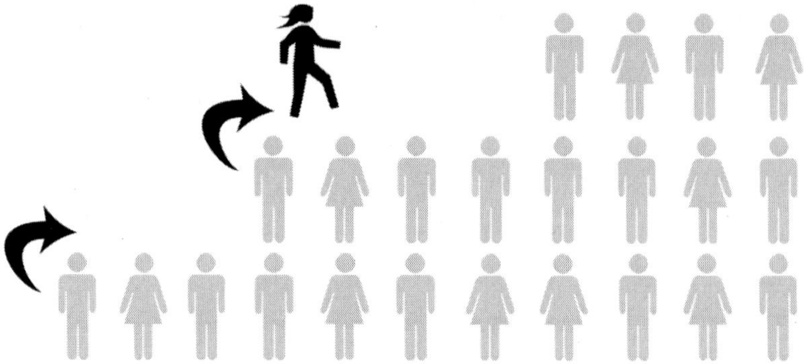

"If I have seen further than others, it is by standing on the shoulders of giants."
—Sir Isaac Newton

It's important to remember the people on our journey who open doors of opportunity for us along the way. The people who recognize our talents, encourage us to pursue our dreams, and connect us to new possibilities are people who deserve some gratitude. World-changers depend on their mentors, coaches, teachers, friends and family members to help guide them on their path. I certainly would not have been able to accomplish any of my goals if it weren't for the encouragers in my life who helped me build my dreams. Saying "thank you" is an easy way to practise kindness and spread some love. I truly believe that we rise by lifting others and that we should always take time to praise fellow world-changers on our journey.

DISCUSSION QUESTIONS

Chapter Eight: The Company You Keep

1) What types of conversations drag down your mood? Why?

2) Make a list of the five people you spend the most time with. Are these people passionate about changing the world just like you?

3) Estimate what percentage of time you spend talking about each of the following topics: people, events and ideas. How can you add more idea-filled conversations into your family and friend circles?

4) Describe a moment where you said or did something wrong. How did you go about fixing the mistake?

5) What qualities would you look for in a partner-in-shine?

6) Who are the people in your life who have been your greatest supporters? Have you told them how much they mean to you?

Challenge for the Week

Show some love and spread some gratitude. Make a point of thanking at least one person each day this week for the value they add to your life. This can be an in-person thank you or a phone call—depending on if they live far away. Avoid sending your thank you through text or email unless there is no other method of contacting the person you are hoping to reach. Suggested people to thank: parents, family members, friends, teachers, coaches, neighbours etc.

CHAPTER 9

Have a Little Faith

"There are two ways to live your life. One is as though nothing is a miracle. The other is as though everything is a miracle."
—Albert Einstein

To have faith is to believe in something larger than yourself. Faith reminds us that we cannot always control the things that happen to us, but we can choose our outlook and how we choose to handle the situations that come our way.

World-changers are fueled by the belief that everything happens for a reason and that even on the darkest days there is a light at the end of the tunnel. No matter which religion or spiritual teaching you follow, or even if you are still seeking, I think all of us can agree that human beings have a desire to connect with something greater than themselves. I think we would all like to believe that someone is watching over us, that there is a plan for the universe and that our lives have a purpose here on earth. To believe in these things is to have faith, and I believe that faith is a necessary ingredient for being a world-changer.

A Sign of Hope

I was raised in a Christian family that believed in having a personal relationship with God. We were encouraged to pray often, to give thanks for our blessings and to live a life filled with service to others. Although I believed in God and in miracles, it wasn't until I had a spiritual encounter at the age of ten that my faith grew to become a central part of my life.

It was late on a Saturday evening in March when my granddad passed away, but I didn't find out until Sunday morning. The words coming from my dad's mouth seemed to slow down and become inaudible as I realized what he was telling me. My body grew very still and I could feel conflicting emotions coming over me. *It couldn't be true, could it? Can people really just disappear and never come back?* The thought of losing my kind, funny and larger-than-life granddad stung my chest and I could feel tears welling up in my eyes. I didn't know what to think.

My dad told me to get dressed to go meet my mom at the children's hospital, where he could tell her the news of Granddad's passing. My mom had been staying at the hospital for almost three months, attending to my six year-old brother who was battling a deadly virus that attacked his brain. About a year before my brother was infected, my granddad had developed acute respiratory distress syndrome (ARDS), a lung condition that prevents enough oxygen from getting to the lungs and into the bloodstream, and was hospitalized in the final months of illness until his death. Indeed, the year 2000 was tough for my family. As a ten year-old child it was devastating to see two close loved ones suffering and not be able to do anything about it.

I sat and thought about memories with my granddad. To me, he was one of the greatest people I had ever known. When he was with me, he treated me like I was the only person in the world. Granddad appreciated the simple things in life and enjoyed spending time outdoors. When I was about seven years old, he planted an evergreen tree seed for me in his front yard. He picked a spot at the far right end of the lawn next to an older evergreen that was so high it looked like it could reach the clouds. Watching my little evergreen tree grow season by season made me very happy. In a way, the two trees seemed to resemble my granddad and me. As the older tree watched the younger one grow tall and strong, my granddad likewise watched over me as I grew.

Granddad also loved birds, and one of his favourite birds was the mallard duck. I remember walking with him along a path by our house that led to a pond filled with ducks and other birds. I was awed by the gorgeous teal colour of the mallard's neck, and I loved watching them gobble down pieces of bread that I threw their way. My granddad loved mallards so much that he carved wooden models of them in his spare time. All around his house my grandma had made room to include his mallard ducks and other bird carvings. Granddad would show me all of his wooden creations from start to finish and I loved how peaceful and calm the carved birds made me feel.

And now here I was, wondering whether I'd ever see my granddad again, in this life or the next. Sure, he wasn't with me right now, but that didn't necessarily mean that he was gone forever. He had to be somewhere, didn't he? Mom and Dad had always talked to me about Heaven and told me that one day we would all be there together. Was it silly to think that my granddad was there in Heaven waiting for me now?

With a slow rhythm I made my bed and went about my morning routine to get ready to visit my brother and mom in the hospital. My sister missed my mom terribly, and being only two years old, she'd often cry out for her. I was walking to find my sister when I heard my father calling me.

"Katie! Come here, quickly!

"Dad?" I called as I turned and started walking down the hallway.

"Hurry! You're not going to believe this!"

I hurried into the living room and saw Dad looking out our front window. He put his finger up to his mouth to signal me to keep quiet, as I gently jumped up on the couch and peered out the window.

"Look there on the driveway," my dad whispered.

There at the end of our driveway was a small figure, moving slowly. It took only a moment for it to turn its head to the side, so I could see the iridescent green colour covering the bird's head. There was no mistaking it; a mallard duck was standing at the edge of our driveway.

I gasped and turned to my dad.

"Daddy, it's him! It's Granddad!"

The duck seemed to stare in our direction. He'd turn his head from side to side every once in a while but his body remained very still.

I jumped off the couch and ran to the front door to get a better look. The duck was still there. I wanted to run to it and hold the duck in my arms. Even from afar, I thought that this was the most beautiful creature I had ever seen. The combinations of colours on the bird's body were stunning. Its gorgeous green head shone in the sun and the bright yellow beak was separated by a dash of royal blue at the front tip. This same blue colour also peeked through the grey feathers in a small patch on the wing.

My dad opened the front door and we stepped onto the porch. The butterflies in my stomach made it difficult for me to stand still as I continued to watch the bird from afar. Even as the duck turned its head from side to side, its eyes never seemed to leave mine. It was as if it wanted to give me enough time to remember every detail of that moment. It felt like a short eternity, a small forever, as I stared transfixed at what I believed to be my granddad's spirit. This recognition calmed my heart and I felt a warm comfort envelope my body. No words could describe the peace I felt in that moment. I was whole and alive all at once.

Then the duck moved. It took three small steps forward on its orange feet, paused for a moment, then opened its beautiful wings and disappeared into the sky.

My dad put his arm around my shoulder and we stood together for a short time. I felt a tear roll down my cheek as I smiled and gave thanks for the moment. I no longer had anything to fear, my granddad was safe and he had come to tell me that he was waiting for me on the other side.

Choose to Believe

Telling this story of my granddad and the mallard duck made me feel vulnerable when I was younger, because sometimes the people I told wouldn't believe me. I could hear their voices trying to fill me with doubt: "That's just a coincidence—birds land on people's driveways all the time. It doesn't mean anything." To which I'd say, "It wasn't just any bird, it was a very specific kind of bird: a mallard duck. Before that day I had never before seen a duck on anyone's driveway, yet alone on my own."

The Oxford English Dictionary defines a miracle as "an extraordinary and welcome event that is not explicable by natural or scientific laws and is therefore attributed to a divine agency." Asking questions about faith and miracles can be a touchy subject. We live in an age and in a country where many people have many faiths, and many other people have no faith at all. You might think that the duck landing on my driveway was just a coincidence, that it was no miracle. I won't blame you—it's hard to fathom. There are some days I even question myself. I'll think, *did that really happen? Is that even possible?* And yes, I have no way of proving that the event was anything more than a coincidence. But whatever we call it, that moment held deep spiritual and personal significance for me. It gave me a feeling I had never experienced before and that I have yet to experience since. It's for this reason that I have chosen to identify the mallard experience as a miracle.

Whether or not you believe in God or a higher power, I want to encourage you to believe in something greater than yourself. Changing the world involves taking risks and helping to build a world that doesn't yet exist. In order to build this world that we seek, we need to have a little faith. You may not see the entire picture but just holding onto a glimmer of hope is enough. Talk to your friends, talk to your families and start having discussions about the blessings and miracles happening in your life. The vastness of the universe, the beauty of a church service, the tenacity of the human spirit—all of these speak of transcendence. The love I had for my granddad, crystallized on that day with the mallard, transcended my normal feelings of existence. Whether you are religious, spiritual or skeptical, I hope that you also experience that same transcendent feeling at some point during your life, as it is truly life-changing. Once you make the decision to live as though everything has a greater purpose, you won't be able to help but see your purpose reflected back to you. As the great Martin Luther King Jr. once said, "Faith is taking the first step even when you don't see the whole staircase."

DISCUSSION QUESTIONS

Chapter Nine: Have a Little Faith

1) What does Albert Einstein's opening quote, "There are two ways to live your life. One is as though nothing is a miracle. The other is as though everything is a miracle," mean to you?

2) How would you define "faith"?

3) Have you ever lost a family member or friend? How did you cope with the loss?

4) Describe a time in your life where you experienced a life-changing event that made you believe in something greater than yourself.

5) Why do you believe that it is important for world-changers to have faith?

Challenge for the Week

Start a conversation with a trusted family member or friend about faith. The goal of this conversation is to get you to think critically about the world around you and your place in it. If you need some help for topics, the questions above serve as great discussion pieces.

CHAPTER 10

Life as a World-Changer

"I don't want to be remembered as the girl who got shot.
I want to be remembered as the girl who stood up."
—Malala Yousafzai

At the end of my Grade Eight year we had the opportunity to answer several questions about ourselves to go beside our picture in the yearbook. There were about ten questions in total and the best answers would be selected for the final printed copy. The questions asked everything from who our favourite teacher was to what our pet peeves were. But the question that really got me thinking was, "What is your ambition?" This question took some deep thought. Some of the kids in my class wrote very specific things like, "Become a doctor," or "Graduate from university"—all great world-changing goals. But I hadn't decided what my specific career would be and felt a little overwhelmed by the idea of having to pick just one thing. And so I dug deep and came up with the best summary I could think of: "To be remembered forever."

Yes, I was *that* girl; the girl who said something so cheesy and "out there" that I could be heavily criticized for it. But maybe our fear of criticism is part of what holds us back from reaching our leadership potential. Our society is quick to tell others that they are dreaming too big or not being realistic. When did it become a taboo thing to talk about wanting to live a great life—a life that has purpose and meaning? I see too many young girls shying away from their full potential because of fear. Fear of failing, fear of what their peers will think and fear of looking too accomplished. Life as a world-changer means breaking the chains of fear and unleashing our unapologetic desire to accomplish great things and change the world. There is a big, delicious greatness pie out there and I promise that there is more than enough for all of us to have a slice. So let's stop telling ourselves that we don't deserve greatness and instead follow our calling as world-changers to make a difference in the lives of others.

So, what do *you* want to be remembered for?

World-Changing Messages

The journey to changing the world is filled with many loops, turns and bumps in the road. To live life as a world-changer we need to keep inspired and keep our eyes on our goals. Below is a summarized list of some of the key messages we have discussed throughout the book thus far:

GIRL TALK PHILOSOPHIES

- ✓ You can be a world-changer right where you are by changing someone else's world for the better.
- ✓ #FirstWorldSolutions is the new #FirstWorldProblems.
- ✓ True beauty is found in living a life of love, kindness and leadership.
- ✓ The best way to find your passions is to follow your curiousity.
- ✓ Leadership is the ability to be a problem solver and a peacemaker simultaneously.
- ✓ Do not compare your behind-the-scenes moments to someone else's highlight reel.
- ✓ Take care of your mind, body and spirit so that you have the strength to change the world.
- ✓ Build your tribe and surround yourself with like-minded world-changers.
- ✓ Have faith that everything happens for a reason.

Acting Locally & Globally

I took a world issues class in high school, hoping to expand my knowledge of politics and current events. One of the first activities we were asked to do in this class was a two-minute mind map of the world. We were handed a blank sheet of paper and told that we had one hundred and twenty seconds to draw an outline of the world map to the best of our ability. I grabbed my pencil and immediately began sketching a rough outline of North America, then South America, then Africa. Then came time to start adding Europe, the Middle East, Asia and Australia.

Wait a minute. This can't be right, I thought. Is Spain really this close to Algeria? Is Saudi Arabia really this close to Sudan? Whenever I would hear people talk of these various countries, I had strong visual images based on pictures I had seen and many of these places felt worlds away from where I was and from each other. How could two countries be so close in proximity and yet be so different? *How sad*, I thought. I wanted to be a human rights advocate and work with global organizations such as the United Nations and yet my knowledge of basic geography was very limited. If I couldn't even find countries on a map, how could I be expected to be a global-minded world-changer?

As world-changers, we need to be passionate about standing up against injustices both in our own communities and on the other side of the planet. And so, I am continually seeking to learn about new places and cultures every day. I consider it our duty to learn more about the world we so desperately want to change. It doesn't take thousands of dollars and a ten-year sailing expedition to learn about the world. You can see the world right where you are by exploring different neighbourhoods, cultures and communities in your own backyard. In my region there are many public events that celebrate the diversity of the community, and I'm sure there are in your community too. These events include multicultural days, parades, fundraisers and religious holiday celebrations. Plus, thanks to technological advances, we have the ability to learn about people on the other side of the planet through formats such as Twitter, documentaries, newspaper articles and high-resolution pictures. I encourage you to make time each day to learn what's making headlines—and what's not—in your community and communities across the globe.

The Girl Who Stood Up

On October 9, 2012, a fifteen year-old girl was shot while travelling home from school in Pakistan. She had been targeted for her work advocating for girls' education and although she had received death threats many times, she chose to continue her mission to change the world. Miraculously, the girl survived and has continued to speak out on the importance of education and human rights. In 2014, she was awarded the Nobel Peace Prize, making history as the youngest person to ever receive this honour. This courageous girl is the ever-inspiring Malala Yousafzai.

Malala has become a powerful force in the girl empowerment movement. She is a shining example of what it means to be a world-changer and an incredible role model for girls and women across the globe. What I love most about Malala's story is that she was just an average fifteen-year old girl who saw an injustice in her community—girls not having the right to go to school—and she decided to do something about it. These are the kinds of stories that we need to be talking about: girls who are truly making a difference in the world. We as world-changers can learn from stories such as Malala's and be inspired to make our own mark.

Make Your Mark

To every girl who has ever wanted to change the world: the time has come for you to take your next step. Gone are the days where we wait for the *somedays* and the *tomorrows* to take action. Gone is the notion that we need to wait until we are more accomplished, more prepared or more likely to change the world. The time to act is now.

Be sure to fill out the Shareable ***"World-Changers Be Like..."*** Pledge located at the back of this book. Then take a picture of yourself holding your pledge and post on social media with the hashtag ***#GIRLTALKBook.***

We look forward to reading your posts and even sharing some stand-outs. ***We will also be spontaneously sending out prizes and GIRL TALK merchandise to some of our favourite pledge-makers!***

At Make Your Mark and GIRL TALK Empowerment, we're building a movement of young people seeking to make the world a better place. The Afterword and last pages of this book are dedicated to sharing more about our movement and how we can keep in-touch. I invite you to connect with us to share your stories, participate in our events and possibly even to start a GIRL TALK Chapter at your school. The possibilities are truly endless and I look forward to seeing where your path takes you.

There has never been a better time to make the leap from your comfort zone and into where the magic happens, than right at this moment. You may be young, but you are powerful. You have the power to change the lives of the people around you with your thoughts, words and actions. Making someone else's day a little brighter with a kind word or a helping hand can change the world. Maybe not the whole world all at once, but certainly their world; and that's world-changing.

> Though she be but little,
> ***she is fierce.***
>
> *-William Shakespeare*

DISCUSSION QUESTIONS
Chapter Ten: Life as a World-Changer

1) How would you answer the question: "What is your ambition?"

2) Do you think girls shy away from wanting to live a great life? Why or why not?

3) Which of the GIRL TALK Philosophies speaks to you the most and why?

4) How can you work to become a more globally-minded leader?

5) The author refers to Malala Yousafzai as an inspiring role model for world-changers. Can you think of any other examples of world-changers who are making the world a better place?

6) What are three ways that you can change the world right now?

Challenge for the Week

Fill out the "World-Changers Be Like" Shareable page located on page 113 then take a picture of you holding your page and post on Facebook, Instagram and/or Twitter with the hashtag #GIRLTALKBook. Consider this your public commitment to being a goal-digging, comfort zone-crushing world-changer. Now it's time for you to take action on your commitment!

AFTERWORD

Creating a GIRL TALK Empowerment Chapter at Your School

If you've taken inspiration from this book, my hope is that you will feel inspired to become more involved in your school and community. I want you to follow your curiousity and chase your passions as you work towards your larger goals. One way to jump into a leadership position and help build a movement is to consider starting a GIRL TALK Empowerment Chapter at your school. There are currently fourteen GIRL TALK Empowerment Chapters in Ontario, and more are being formed all the time! This section is dedicated to sharing more about the GIRL TALK Empowerment movement and how you can take the lead right where you are.

About GIRL TALK Empowerment

Our Mission: To unite and empower girls to make their mark on the world.

Our Vision: To spark a movement of confident, passionate and empowered girls who are committed to making a difference in the lives of others.

What is GIRL TALK Empowerment Day? GIRL TALK Empowerment Day, or #GIRLTALKDay as it's known on social media, is a one-day pep rally dedicated to motivating girls to take local and global action through musical performances and story sharing. This feature event currently takes place annually in the Greater Toronto Area, with plans to expand to more cities in the near future. Watch videos from GIRL TALK Empowerment Day online on YouTube by searching "GIRL TALK Empowerment."

Why Start a GIRL TALK Chapter?

- ✓ Give yourself and others an opportunity to take leadership roles within your school
- ✓ Get girls in your school involved in important issues related to building self-esteem, positive body image, leadership and standing up to bullying
- ✓ Receive videos, event ideas and other resources throughout the year
- ✓ Save money on GIRL TALK events and merchandise

What Our Current GIRL TALK School Chapters Have Been Up To:

- ♥ Clothing drive for a local women's shelter
- ♥ Pink t-shirt day against bullying
- ♥ Mental health awareness campaign
- ♥ Zumba fitness day
- ♥ Positive post-it note campaign on school lockers
- ♥ Mentoring younger girls at school
- ♥ Bake sale raising money for an underprivileged family
- ♥ Yoga and healthy-eating workshops
- ♥ Weekly support groups

What Does the Commitment Look Like?

- All we ask is that registered schools host at least one girl empowerment event throughout the school year (of course, we encourage you to do more than one, but hosting even one event will give you access to all of the GIRL TALK Chapter benefits).

- Each school has the freedom to choose how they organize the GIRL TALK group at their school. Some schools may choose to run an ongoing support system; others may choose to host mini events throughout the school year etc.

Already have several leadership and human rights clubs at your school?
Your GIRL TALK Chapter could be a branch of a larger cause or group. One of our 2014-2015 School Chapters decided to start a "Make Your Mark" group at their school (which served as an "umbrella committee," overseeing all school leadership activities,) and then registered a GIRL TALK Chapter as an off-shoot of this main Make Your Mark leadership team.

Keeping In-Touch with the GIRL TALK Empowerment Team

Our GIRL TALK Empowerment team is committed to supporting you on your journey to build a successful GIRL TALK Chapter at your school. Our goal is to have on-going communication with you and your team to ensure that you have all of the tools you need to make a BIG impact.

Our Commitment to You: We plan to connect with you through email at least once a month with some inspiration and ideas to help keep your momentum going. We are also available throughout the year via social media, email or phone for questions, concerns and support.

The GIRL TALK Chapter Awards

In June 2015, GIRL TALK launched its first ever Chapter Awards ceremony at the 3rd Annual GIRL TALK Empowerment Day in Oshawa, Ontario. This initiative was created to recognize the outstanding work of the girls, teachers and schools who have committed to leading a GIRL TALK School Chapter. The awards included: Most School Spirit, School of the Year and five individual GIRL TALK Champion awards. The GIRL TALK Chapter Awards are now an annual event and online applications open in April each year.

Registering a GIRL TALK School Chapter is easy.
Visit ***girltalkempowerment.com*** and highlight the ***"Resources"*** tab, then click ***"Start a GIRL TALK Chapter."***

Upon submitting your form someone will be in-touch from our team shortly to discuss further details.

CONNECT

With Katie Zeppieri & GIRL TALK

KATIE ZEPPIERI	GIRL TALK EMPOWERMENT
katiezeppieri.com	girltalkempowerment.com
/katie.zeppieri.page	/girltalkempowerment
@KatieZeppieri	@GIRLTALKEmpower
@KatieZeppieri	@GIRLTALKEmpowerment
Katie Zeppieri	GIRL TALK Empowerment

#GIRLTALKBook

WORLD-CHANGERS BE LIKE...

My name is ______________________________
and today I am committing to being a

GOAL-DIGGING,
COMFORT ZONE-CRUSHING,
WORLD-CHANGER.

HERE ARE THREE WAYS I AM GOING TO START CHANGING THE WORLD:

1) ______________________________
2) ______________________________
3) ______________________________

I AIN'T NOTHING BUT A GOAL-DIGGER AND YOU CAN BE TOO.

WHO'S WITH ME?

#GIRLTALKBook

ACKNOWLEDGEMENTS

Writing *GIRL TALK* has been one of the most honest, reflective, challenging and rewarding experiences of my life. I want to extend my deepest gratitude to the people who have helped make me the person I am today. This book would not have been possible without a team of inspiring world-changers who I am proud to call my tribe.

Mom, thank you for being my rock. I remember being a little girl watching you speak in front of crowds and making a difference in the community, thinking to myself, *I hope to be just like my mom someday.*

Dad, thank you for being the anchor of our family and the moral compass I turn to for direction. You were my greatest fan even in the lowest moments and for this I am forever grateful.

Brandon and Emily, thank you for being the ever-entertaining sibling duo who never lets me take myself too seriously and who always makes me laugh. It is inspiring to see you both chasing your passions and following your dreams. Shout out to Emily for doing my hair & makeup for the cover photos.

Grandma and Nonna, thank you for sharing your stories and wisdom with me. I'm grateful for your love, support and active presence in my life.

Granddad, Nonno, Great Nana and Great Grandpa who passed too soon, we miss you dearly. Granddad, you always told me that someday I'd be a writer and I'm proud to have seen this dream come to life.

Shawn, editing this book is just one example of your many talents being used to support my dreams. Thank you for being my partner-in-shine. I look forward to changing the world with you.

Family and Friends, thank you for your boosts of encouragement and kind expressions of love throughout my journey.

Madison, thank you not only for designing the covers and the layout of this book but also for helping me build GIRL TALK from a single event to a growing movement. You're a dedicated teammate and a great friend.

Alishba from Purple Canvas Photography, thank you for taking the amazing photos for the cover of this book. (The balloon pose might have hurt a little, but it was worth it!)

Former Principals/Teachers/Secretaries/Coaches/Mentors, thank you for opening doors of opportunity for me and for giving me nuggets of wisdom during some of the most difficult moments of my journey.

GIRL TALK Empowerment Board & Volunteers, thank you for volunteering your time, energy and resources to help support a movement I am so deeply passionate about. Our events couldn't run without talented, dedicated, world-changing people like you taking the lead.

ABOUT THE AUTHOR

Having developed an entrepreneurial spirit at a young age, Katie Zeppieri is proud to be the Founder & Chief Empowerment Officer of Make Your Mark, a social enterprise that provides leadership development training to youth. She is also the Founder of GIRL TALK Empowerment, a movement dedicated to motivating girls to become leaders of positive change.

Katie's outspoken voice has led her to travel across Canada and abroad to speak about issues that matter. She is a motivational speaker, who has spoken on many platforms, including on the TED Worldwide Stage, a blogger for The Huffington Post, an on-air radio panelist Monday mornings on NEWSTALK 1010 with Host, Jerry Agar, a YouTube vlogger, and a journalist who has had her work featured in such outlets as Forbes.com. Katie is a champion for human rights and gained her passion for speaking out after both witnessing and experiencing many forms of bullying during her school years.

Katie graduated from high school in 2007 as a Top 20 Under 20 Finalist, a recipient of the prestigious TD Canada Trust $60,000 Scholarship for "Community Leadership" and was awarded the Governor General's "Caring Canadian" Award. She is a YMCA Peace Medallion Recipient, a June Callwood Harmony Scholarship Recipient and has been recognized by the YWCA as a "Young Woman of Distinction." Katie has also made her mark in the pageant world having been crowned "Miss Italia" and "Miss Fiesta" in her local community and then placing as the 3rd Runner-up in the 2013 Miss World Canada pageant.

Katie is dedicated to promoting leadership, encouraging young people to have a positive self-image and standing up against injustices. She hopes to use her leadership background to mentor and empower an entire generation of youth to "make their mark" on the world.